PRACTICAL SOCCER TACTICS

For Youth Coaches

by Larry Maisner
Foreword by Don Greer

 WORLD

World Publications, Inc.
Mountain View, California

Recommended Reading:
Soccer World Magazine, $7.50/year
Write Box 366, Mt. View, CA 94042,
for a free catalog of publications.

Library of Congress Cataloging in Publication Data

Maisner, Larry, 1931-
    Practical soccer tactics.

    1. Soccer coaching. I. Title
GV943.8.M33   796.33'42   78-64382
ISBN 0-89037-157-1

World Publications
Mountain View, CA

Table of Contents

Foreword

As the United States progresses with its developing soccer program, the final step will be the teaching of tactics to our players. Once our players are able to master this important phase of the game, the U.S. will begin to take its place alongside other great soccer countries of the world.

As Larry Maisner points out, tactical awareness can only start to develop in a meaningful way after match fitness and ball skills have matured. We are at that point now in this country. Tactics are the fine points of the game—intelligent use of tactics is the mark of a well-coached player because only a rare few pick up tactical awareness on their own—some players never get a grasp for it.

That is why *Practical Soccer Tactics* is such a vital and timely book. Here is virtually everything youth teams could hope to learn about the thinking side of the game, set forth in an elementary style that will make it very useful for youth coaches to teach tactics as a regular phase of their practices. With this step, American teams will begin to play soccer on par with the best teams in the world.

Don Greer

Chairman
United States
Youth Soccer
Association

Introduction

A well-known South American soccer coach visited these shores recently to lecture American youth soccer coaches. I was fortunate to attend one of his seminars and to hear him discuss the structure of soccer organizations in his native land, the need for physical conditioning, the importance of ball-skills training, and the promise of soccer as a big-time sport in America.

He showed a film of a World Cup match and pointed out the strengths and weaknesses of each play. He talked about match preparation and several other important topics. But not once did he mention tactics.

Finally, a coach in the audience challenged him on this curious omission. "Tactics," our lecturer answered, "are not learned at a seminar, they are learned on a soccer pitch. Unlike American football, you cannot coach tactics with a chalkboard because soccer tactics are too variable." He further defended his omission by saying, "When you talk of tactics, you must specify what kind of tactics you are talking about: defensive, offensive, team, etcetera. Each is a subject by itself."

Our guest lecturer was right on all counts, but only to a point. His level of expertise was so far above his audience that he could not recognize our need for even the most basic information on tactics. For him, the fundamental tactical ploys players use are second nature and need no explanation.

But there *are* standard tactics that should be learned at the youth soccer level. True, tactical concepts are not easily learned from the chalkboard or even from this book. This book has been designed to guide the youth soccer coach in teaching fundamental soccer tactics *on the field*. With the help of the drills and practice techniques that follow, you, as a coach, can greatly increase the tactical awareness of your players. The burden will be on you to make these subtle concepts second nature to your players in the great variety of situations they will encounter on the playing field.

Tactics:

The Fingerprints of Soccer

Exactly what does the youth soccer coach teach his students? He has three areas of responsibility: the development and maintenance of physical fitness, the acquisition of ball skills, and the generation of tactical awareness. Players are ready for productive tactical training only when they:

1. have sufficient skills to control the ball under moderate pressure while thinking about the next play,

2. are sufficiently fit to keep control of the ball when fatigued,

3. realize that soccer, beyond the familiar dimensions of the ball and the other players, has the dimensions of space and time.

Physical fitness is paramount in importance. Without it, players are unable to use their skills effectively or to maintain pressure on the opposing team. Ball skills are those techniques players use as individuals to win and control the ball. Tactics are methods that individual players, groups of players, or entire teams use to execute plays. Tactics provide the "fingerprint" of a team; that is, a team is distinguished by the way its players plan and carry out their jobs on the field of play.

The Three T's of Soccer

The three T's of soccer are Technique, Tactics, and Training. Modern coaching methods combine acquisition of ball skills

1

(technique), development of the playing arts (tactics), and physical fitness maintenance into an economical training program. That is, players get and keep fit by doing drills designed to develop ball skills and tactical awareness at the same time.

Employment of these methods is the heart of practical youth soccer coaching: advancing a team to its peak of competitive condition in the shortest time possible, with the facilities and equipment available.

Teaching Tactics

The facilities available to the youth soccer coach are very limited in most communities. Also, a youth soccer coach usually has only so much time that can be devoted to the team. Efficient use is made of precious practice time when players receive their conditioning during skill drills. The economical training program stresses progressive training principles (detailed in chapter 6). Briefly, to give the training program maximum effect. the youth soccer coach must:

1. Pre-plan each practice session in terms of the team's immediate needs. In this way, idle time is held to a minimum, and the training is devoted to specific areas.

2. Simulate match pace and procedure in all drills. The closer the dynamics of the practices to the dynamics of competition, the sooner a team will reach match fitness.

3. Design drills for work group balance so that all players get as many touches on the ball as possible. Sharpness of ball control is directly related to the number of times a player is in possession of the ball. Tactics cannot be taught efficiently when a player still has to concentrate on ball control.

4. Make drills competitive and fun. Youngsters are far more willing to work hard if they see an objective: to keep possession of the ball, to beat a teammate to a loose ball, to complete more passes than any other teammate, and so on.

5. Increase competitive pressure steadily until the team can handle match pressures. Match pressures include challenge, space restriction, time restriction, and fatigue.

THE YOUNG PLAYER

The coach of young soccer players must deal with physical and mental faculties that differ markedly from year to year, whereas the coach of adult players deals with faculties that stay fairly uniform. A college soccer coach asked to take over a "peewee" team would have much to get accustomed to. The physical and intellectual differences between the two age groups are so great that substantially different coaching methods are required.

From the time a youngster can learn soccer in an organized way until he is fully equipped for competitive soccer, he is continuously growing physically and mentally. As a rule, it is not practical to coach teams where the players' age differences are more than about two years. It is impractical to teach an eleven-year-old the same things at the same rate as a fourteen-year-old. Bearing in mind that an occasional player may be advanced for his age, the coach must make certain his instructions are geared to the age level of his players.

The length of time that a child can concentrate on a thought or activity keeps increasing until it peaks out, usually during his mid-teens. Generally, the younger the players, the more difficult it is to hold their attention.

The youth soccer coach's worst enemy is distraction from activity near his practice area. The ideal time for practice, then, is when no other teams are in the area. Drills should be kept fairly short; very young players will probably lose attention after a dozen or so repetitions.

A coach must adapt the language he uses to the level of the players. Very young players are unfamiliar with terms commonly used in soccer. Moreover, they do not understand vocabulary used by more mature junior players and adults. The youth soccer coach must get his message across by being patient, demonstrating instead of instructing, and not taking understanding for granted.

PLANNING THE PRACTICE SESSION

Coaches must be miserly with the time available for team practice. There should be nonactive time only when planned, such as for short discussions which double as rest periods. Players not actively working with the ball should be analyzing the activity of players who are, under supervision of an assistant coach.

The most important item to cover is always the correction of mistakes made in the last match. Second priority should be any items scheduled but not covered in the previous practice session. The schedule should be flexible enough to allow time to see that the problem solution is working and that the team sees it working too. If the time needed to solve a problem will affect the schedule adversely, it may be necessary to schedule a special practice session just for that problem.

Above all, the practices must be designed to meet the particular needs of the players as individuals, groups, and as a team. For example, if a player is having trouble with the give-and-go pass, the drills he works in should emphasize use of that technique. Similarly, if the team is being scored on heavily, concentration should be on defensive drills.

SIMULATING MATCH PACE

All drills should simulate match pace; that is, spurts of intense activity sandwiched between longer periods of moderately paced activity. That is the pace a soccer player's blood circulation and respiratory system must adjust to. This mixture of intense and relaxed activity is widely known as "interval training."

Interval training decreases the amount of time it takes for an athlete to recover from intense activity. Throughout a match players must chase at high speed while defending or dribble at high speed while attacking, then patrol while finding or maintaining their effective field position. The match-fit player can chase or dribble at high speed whenever necessary; the less-than-fit player needs time to recover before being able to chase or dribble at high speed again.

All things done on the practice field should simulate match procedure. A ball thrown to a player casually should be trapped rather than caught. Laps run around the practice field should be made while dribbling a ball. As a practical matter, the players should run in small groups, each player in a group taking a turn with the ball, since there is not likely to be one practice ball per player. These good training habits pave the way for good tactical training habits, such as running in close support of the ball carrier or sprinting on recovery runs.

WORK GROUP BALANCE

The size of the work group and the area assigned for the work are two important considerations in tactical practices. If the group is too large, each player will not get enough touches on the ball for the drill to be effective. If the group is too small, the realism of the drill will be lost.

The size of the work area should be related to the size of the work group and the quality of the players' ball skills. Not all team drills need be played on a full field (often a full field is not available anyway). A full team scrimmage can be played effectively across half a field, using markers for goal posts.

The smaller the area assigned, the greater the demand for precise ball control. The players are close together, so a poorly trapped ball that bounces loose, for example, will likely be won by a close-by challenger. Small-sided games and drills involving as many as eight players with moderate ball skills can be played in a quarter of a field. And the area can be further reduced as skill levels rise.

COMPETITION IN PRACTICE

Most youngsters are naturally competitive, some more so than others. When assigning players to competitive drills, differences in competitive levels must be considered in order to avoid bruised egos and to keep the competition realistically even.

The coach who is doing the right things with his team will see the quality of his players' skills rise rapidly. But performance is really only measurable by the ratio of success to failure; as a player does more things right than wrong, he achieves more on the field of play. Without competition in practice, a coach cannot monitor performance realistically, so he must place practices in realistic situations. For example, wall-passing drills for experienced players should be carried out under pressure from a challenger; group striking drills should finish with a shot on goal if the attack is successful or a placed clearance if the defense is successful; the defenders in a defensive team drill should be awarded points for winning the ball from the offensive players, with the same number of points being awarded to the offensive players for a successful strike.

HANDLING PRESSURE

Tactical drills should be done under little or no pressure until the players gain confidence in controlling the ball and are able to see the tactic work successfully. The pressures should then be increased until the players can perform the tactic under full match pressure. If the players are constantly frustrated in their efforts to complete the tactic being drilled, the drill is not achieving its objective: to show the players that it does work and how.

Behavioral Tactics

Tactics are not only the ways plays are physically executed. They include the spirit in which plays are executed. Positive attitudes and behavior are important allies of soccer skills.

TALKING PLAYS

Soccer is one of the most team-oriented sports, but some soccer matches (notably junior games) are played in silence. This should not be so. It indicates a lack of tactical understanding, a lack of team spirit, or both.

Players should talk positively to each other at every opportunity. That means encouraging, complimenting, and instructing teammates; it does not mean criticizing teammates. That is the coach's job, off the field of play.

Encouraging and complimentary remarks reinforce team spirit, particularly if a team is under pressure. They have a positive effect on all players within earshot. On the other hand, criticisms turn off team spirit. Players should ignore their teammates' mistakes; players busy with their own game cannot tell the difference between unavoidable failures and careless failures.

Instructions are even more valuable than compliments in encouraging successful team play. A dribbler often cannot see potential dangers or playmaking possibilities as well as a nearby teammate can. That teammate can warn the dribbler of danger or point out a play for him. For example, the dribbler might be warned of a challenger approaching on his blind side by a quick "man on you!" Or, a winger might be made aware of a good scoring chance by the shout "center!" from an inside forward near the goalmouth.

THINKING POSITIVELY

Positive thinking is a lot of healthy attitudes in a player about his capabilities rolled up in the conviction that he can achieve his objective regardless of the competition. It is not simply confidence—a realist's confidence will break down in the face of demonstrated superiority. The expression "he didn't know how tough it was to do, so he went ahead and did it anyway" is a good example of positive thinking. It begins with the conviction that success is likely despite common-sense odds.

Probably the most important time for a player to apply positive thinking is when competing for a loose ball. Say the competing players are about equal distances from the ball, have comparable skills, and are about as strong and fast as each other. Who will win the ball? The last-minute doubts of the less-than-positive thinker will create a play-destroying hesitation as he closes on the ball with his competitor. On the other hand, the conviction of the positive thinker will allow him to use all his faculties to the fullest extent, and he wins the ball.

The youth soccer coach particularly must continually emphasize and reinforce positive thinking in his players. At the same time, he must beware of causing cockiness or brashness. Such unwholesome attitudes can easily replace positive thinking if success goes to players' heads. No one is successful all the time, but the edge goes to positive thinkers more often than to less-than-positive thinkers.

2

Systems of Play

Many systems of play (team formations) have been developed, tried, discarded, or improved over the years. Only a few have really withstood the test of time. The rest have defects fatal to effective soccer, especially youth soccer.

Systems are described by a three-part number that gives the location of players' field positions at kickoff time. The first number indicates the number of fullbacks, the second the number of halfbacks, and the third the number of forwards. (The goalkeeper is not included in the number because he is in the same position, regardless of the system used.) Probably the most commonly used systems for youth teams are the 2-3-5, 3-3-4, and 4-2-4.

There are twelve identifiable playing positions. Most of these positions have more than one name. The playing positions, player names, and general traits suitable for the various positions are listed in table 1.

System Selection

Youth coaches seldom have the chance to scout for talent to fill particular field positions. Those that do are fairly free to choose the type of system they wish to work with. Those that do not must build a system around the talent available. For example, the coach with plenty of forward talent but few skillful defenders should adopt a 2-3-5 system (see fig. 1). The coach with few good forwards but lots of defensive talent should select

Table 1. Player Position Characteristics

Field Positions	Player Name	Player Type
Forward:		
Wings	Outside right (OR), outside left (OL), right winger, left winger.	Fastest players, good balance, able to change pace and direction fast, strong right foot for OR, strong left foot for OL.
Central	Inside forward, inside right (IR), inside left (IL), striker.	Good ball control, willing to set up players, good right foot for IR, good left foot for IL.
Center	Center forward (CF), striker.	Tall, fast, good ball control. Good shot with either foot, good head shot.
Midfield:		
Wings	Right halfback (RH), left halfback (LH), wing halfback, linkman, midfielder.	Able to control ball fast from air, good at both offense and defense, high work rate capability.
Central	Center halfback (CH), center half, midfielder.	Tall, aggressive, plenty of stamina, leadership capability, good playmaker, strong tackler.
Backfield:		
Wings	Right fullback (RB), left fullback (LB), wing fullback.	Aggressive tacklers, persistent, strong right foot for RB, strong left foot for LB.
Central	Center fullback (CB).	Aggressive tackler, persistent, two-footed, fast, strong heading capability, disciplined and cool position player.
Deep central	Sweeper (libero).	Aggressive tackler, persistent, fastest defender, experienced in all phases of soccer.

either a 3-3-4 (see fig. 2) or 4-2-4 (see fig. 3) system.

The ideal system for very young players, as well as older youth players with limited skills, is the 3-3-4 system, for several reasons. First, it provides a balanced coverage of the playing field—no player has to work harder than any other at controlling his area of the field. Second, it is effective in controlling midfield, so that no excessive pressure is placed on the defense or the offense. Finally, it provides a "spine" of strength down the middle of the field; the area in which youngsters have the best chance of building up effective attacks and defenses.

As players grow older, stronger, and more experienced, the 2-3-5 and 4-2-4 systems become more practical for the coach with the player talent to handle them. For the offensively ori-

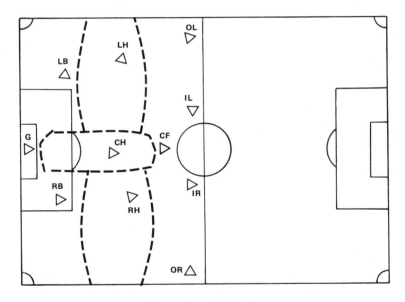

Figure 1. 2-3-5 System

Offense: 1) Powerful attack if properly coordinated.
          2) Often at least one forward extra on any strike.

Midfield: 1) Must be expert defensively to relieve pressure on fullbacks.
          2) Must be good playmakers to select pass options to numerous forwards.
          3) Strong midfield advantage if CH can work effectively with CF.

Fullbacks: 1) Must be fast, have high work rate, be expert, and work well with goalie.
           2) When in control of ball, they have many options for playmaking and must clear ball from defense area fast.

ented 2-3-5 system, forwards must be able to coordinate attacks without wasting the presence of one or more players, and full-backs must be fast, determined, and must work well with an experienced goalie. The more defensively oriented 4-2-4 system needs two tireless and expert halfbacks and well-coordinated fullbacks.

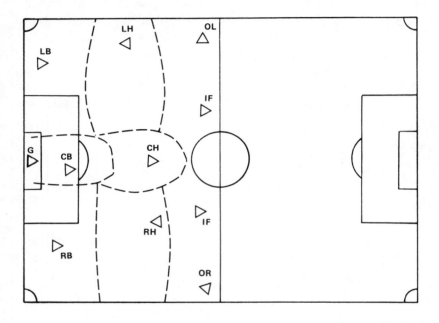

Figure 2. 3-3-4 System

Offense: 1) Requires good understanding of playing ball into space behind opposing defense.
              2) Wingers must be able to draw opposing defense from center of goalmouth.
              3) Usually good scoring chances through service from midfield.

Midfield: 1) Exceptional strength at midfield through connection of CH and inside forwards.
              2) If wing halves are weak, they are well backed up by wing fullbacks.

Fullbacks: 1) Strong direct coverage of defense area by CB.
              2) Backup for wing fullbacks from CB, whose position can be covered by CH.

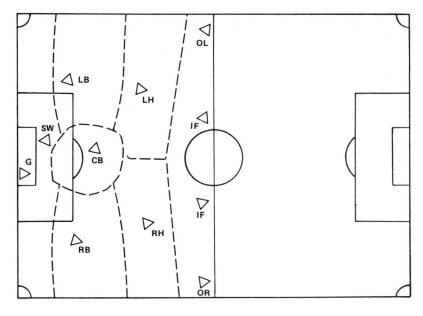

Figure 3. 4-2-4 System

Offense: 1) Requires good understanding of playing ball into space behind opposing defense.
           2) Will have to work hard to win ball and create scoring chances because of thin midfield support.

Midfield: 1) Large area to cover makes midfield control difficult.
           2) High work rate capability essential. Must be aggressive and expert on both offense and defense.

Fullbacks: 1) Provide exceptionally strong defense, particularly if one fullback is used as a sweeper (SW), (1-2-3-4 System).
           2) Will be under pressure more often due to difficulty in controlling midfield.

System Mobility

On paper, systems of play look neat and practical. However, in match situations their starting pattern lasts for only a few seconds following the kickoff. Experienced teams will maintain the very general pattern of their system during play (even though players may interchange positions). Less experienced teams will quickly lose the starting pattern of the system through lack of mobility or, conversely, through excessive mobility. The importance of system mobility is covered in greater detail in chapter 3.

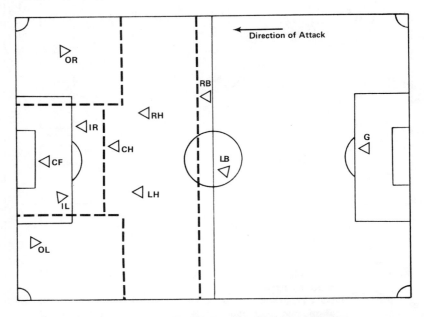

Figure 4. Areas of Control for Players on Attack in a 2-3-5 System

3

The Players' Roles in Tactics

Though individual, group, and team tactics are basically distinct, there is one tactical concept that is fundamental to all three: all players must be doing something all the time. All players must be doing offensive things when their team has the ball. All players must be doing defensive things when the opposing team has the ball.

Being idle is boring for players and counterproductive to their game. It causes mental and physical inertia, that is, difficulty getting their minds and bodies up to speed again after having been idle. Players should be reminded frequently and emphatically that there is always something constructive to do in the field of play, whether the ball is near them or not—even if the ball is out of play.

Individual Tactics

Each player on a team has a primary job and a secondary job. The primary job is challenging for the ball or carrying it. The secondary job is supporting a teammate who is engaged in the primary job. These concepts apply equally to forwards, midfielders, fullbacks, and goalies.

The three distinct tactical units, as described in chapter 2, are forwards, midfielders or halfbacks, and fullbacks. In more advanced tactics, the roles of these players often overlap. In basic tactical training, it is advisable to coach players fairly rigidly for their specific roles because they will not yet be equipped to handle more than one role at a time. The "classic" roles of players in their assigned positions are listed in table 2.

BALL RETENTION

A player is a ball hog when he keeps the ball even though an open and visible teammate has a better chance of making a play. He is a play destroyer when he has a good chance of penetrating a defense alone but passes the ball to a teammate who has less chance. He is a team player when he understands what a ball hog and a play destroyer are, and acts like neither of them.

A ball hog is not necessary being greedy. He may have no choice. His teammates may have let him down by not positioning themselves for a pass, by not seeking a better playmaking chance, or by not calling for the ball.

A play destroyer is not necessarily lacking in character. He may lack the confidence to beat a challenger because his coach has not yet taught him sound dribbling technique. Or, his coach may have overemphasized the importance of passing at all costs.

There is no rule of thumb for how long a player should retain the ball before passing it. The only certainty is that he has held it too long if he loses it. If players are losing the ball to challengers, some possible problems are:

1. Inferior dribbling technique. Either they cannot beat their man in a one-on-one confrontation, or they cannot dribble while watching their immediate surroundings. Extra training in dribbling skills is required.

2. They have inferior support. (This problem is dealt with under "Supporting Roles" in this chapter.)

3. They are ball hogs because they are greedy. This is a tricky problem to deal with. A coach must insist that they become conscious of other members of the team. A good demonstration for a ball hog is to have him dribble the ball from the 18-yard line to the center line of the field while the team counts

Table 2. Players' Positional Responsibilities

Player	Responsibility
Forwards:	
Winger	Controls area from touchline to edge of opposing penalty area, and from opposing goal line to about first third of field (fig. 4). Draws defenders from center of field to give inside forwards attacking space. Often takes corner kicks.
Inside Forward	Together with center forward, controls central forward area. Combines with center forward for penetrating plays. Often uses winger for penetration when goal area tightly defended. Together with center forward, has the most chances for effective shot making.
Center Forward	Has the best chance to be most productive scorer. Works closely with inside forwards for defense penetration. Usually in best position for scoring with head or feet from wing passes.
Midfielders:	
Wing Half	Best source of connecting passes from defense to wing forwards. First line of defense against opposing inside forwards. Cover for own wing fullbacks if needed. (Note that midfielders play an important dual role as supporters in both defense and offense.)
Center Half	Central ball distributor for all forwards. Often used as an extra inside forward if opposing goal area is loosely defended. First line of defense against attacking center forward. Cover for own center fullbacks if needed.
Defenders:	
Wing Fullback	Primary defense against attacking wing forward or wing half. Defensive tactics are to keep attackers contained in touchline area, and tackle for possession when backed up by support.
Center Fullback	Primary defense against attacking center forward/inside forward combinations. Also, will act as support behind containing wing fullback if no sweeper available. Defensive tactics are to keep striker from having unpressured shot on goal, and tackle for possession when backed up by sweeper.
Sweeper	Utility defender. May be free center fullback in four-fullback system. Supports defense by staying closely behind challenging fullback and collecting (sweeping) loose ball if challenging fullback is beaten. Also covers space behind fullbacks to discourage long through pass plays by attackers.
Goalkeeper	Last line of defense against shots on goal. His ability to use hands for ball control in penalty area makes him useful as an extra "fullback" for setting up fast counterattacks.

the elapsed seconds. Then have him kick a ball from the 18-yard line to a teammate on the center line while the team counts the elapsed seconds. The time difference should impress him.

SUPPORTING ROLES

A player's mission is one of direct support if a nearby teammate has the ball. To support the ball carrier directly, a player must run with the carrier. The support player is said to be "running off the ball" (or running without the ball). The player running off the ball must position himself so that the ball carrier can see him, and so that the nearest defender cannot intercept a pass.

Pass target. The player running off the ball may have to call loudly to the ball carrier. The ball carrier is often concentrating on keeping control of the ball under pressure and may see the pass opportunity only if he is alerted.

To avoid pass interception, the player running off the ball must be sure a clear path exists for the pass to reach him and that no nearby defender has a chance to beat him to the ball. He does this by moving to a position where he, the ball carrier, and the defending challenger form a triangle (see fig. 5). The support player can then receive either a square pass or a through pass. The square pass travels more or less laterally to the receiver and across the front of the challenger. The through pass travels past the challenger to, or beyond, the receiver.

If the player challenging the ball carrier sees the carrier's support moving into open space to receive a pass, the challenger will try to position himself to cut off the pass. Therefore, the support player should run into passing space when the challenger's attention is riveted on the ball carrier.

As soon as the ball carrier has passed the ball to his supporting teammate, he should take over the support role if no other teammate does. As shown in figure 5, the player passing the ball to his teammate immediately runs to space where he is open for a return pass. Inexperienced players must be trained to understand that their job continues after a completed pass—but in a support role.

If a teammate has the ball and is not nearby, a support player should be looking for running space in which to collect a

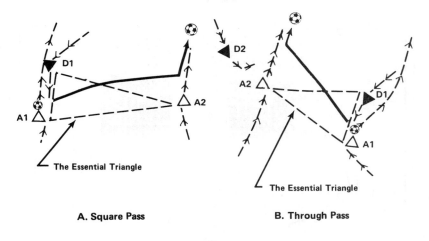

A. Square Pass   B. Through Pass

Figure 5. Basic Passing Patterns

long pass. However, very young players, because they cannot send the ball very far very accurately, need to maintain close support.

Defensive support. Defending players support a challenging teammate by covering or marking likely pass targets. Or, should the challenging teammate go into a tackle, one would play back up. If the opposing ball carrier is not nearby, a supporting defender covers all possible pass targets in his zone.

Decoy runs. Decoy runs lure a defender away from productive running space for the ball carrier or collecting space for a pass receiver. The decoy player knows he will not be directly involved in ball contact. Such a tactic involves a sacrifice that less mature youngsters are not always willing to make. But decoy runs play a critical part in opening up penetration chances for teammates.

A typical decoy play is shown in figure 6. Before the play starts, attackers A4 and A5 are well covered, and there are no good chances to penetrate the defense. The attacker with the deepest position and least cover is A2. With the smart decoy running of A3, this is how penetration could be achieved:

1. Attacker A1 serves the ball to A2. A2 holds the ball and draws defender D2 towards him for challenge.

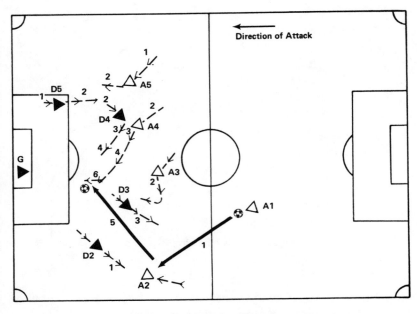

Figure 6. Decoy Running

2. A3, who is covered by D3, runs toward A2 while signaling for a square pass. But A2, though he might fake a pass, continues to hold the ball.

3. Defender D3 "buys" the square pass signals given by A3 and moves into position for an interception.

4. Once D3 commits, A4 sprints toward point X to offer a pass target. If A4 had started his run earlier, D3 would have been alerted and would not have been decoyed out of position.

5. A2 sees A4 start his sprint and serves the ball to point X.

6. With a substantial lead on D4, A4 collects the ball and starts a relatively unpressured strike on goal.

Small-sided games and restart drills are ideal for developing decoy run instincts. These activities give a coach the chance to work close in with his players and encourage "free" off-the-ball players to isolate opponents from potential penetration space.

Selling the dummy. A player can become a hero or a dunce in the short time it takes to miss collecting a pass. A hero might purposely miss a pass, letting it continue to a supporting teammate, in order to draw an opponent toward him and away from the teammate who has more open running room with the ball. The opponent is called the "buyer" of the dummy. The tactic is a short-term decoy run, as shown in figure 7.

Figure 7a shows an offensive sale. The seller fakes a collection of the ball. The buyer commits himself to a tackle. The ball goes past the seller and the buyer to the now open supporting teammate.

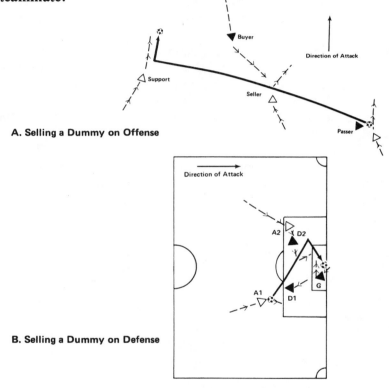

A. Selling a Dummy on Offense

B. Selling a Dummy on Defense

Figure 7. Selling the Dummy

A similar sale is shown in figure 7b, except the sale is defensive and the seller is his own support. Attacker A1 has served a through pass for A2 to collect and strike. Defender D2 recovers quickly enough to fake an interception of the pass, and A2 swerves to challenge the interception. Defender D2 lets the ball continue, turns, and feeds the ball back to his keeper from a less hazardous position.

OVERLAPPING AND RECOVERY RUNS

On an overlapping run, a fullback passes his midfielders or even his forwards to receive a pass from behind, often with the possibility of a strike on goal. Likewise, a midfielder might pass his forwards on an overlapping run. Whenever a player makes an overlapping run, his teammates must be prepared to cover his position quickly if the ball turns over to the opposition.

One drawback of overlapping runs is the intense physical demands they place on the overlapping player. He runs at high speed for unusually long distances and must return quickly to his regular position. The returning run is called a "recovery run." Any coach who employs this tactic must make certain his team is (1) capable of covering unaccustomed open zones when needed, and (2) fit enough to run the length of the field twice at sprint pace, with enough energy left to play the rest of the match at competitive speeds.

These conditions are tough but well worth the effort to achieve them. Overlapping runs can demolish the opposition. An intelligent decoy run by an overlapping fullback can put unmanageable pressure on an opponent's defense. For instance, in

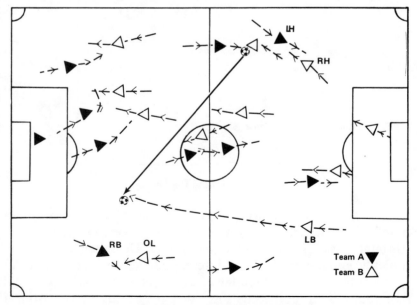

Figure 8. Overlapping Run on Weakened Side of Field

figure 8 the team B halfback (RH) has just won the ball from the team A halfback. The offensive players draw their opponents toward the right side of the field, creating a weak side on the left. (Team B winger OL, however, decoys fullback RB toward the left-hand touchline.) These maneuvers leave a useful lane down the left-central part of the field, which the team B left fullback can exploit with an overlapping run. Notice that since play is predominantly on the right side, the left fullback is substantially free of defensive responsibilities. The halfback in possession serves the ball ahead of the fullback for him to collect and strike on goal.

Opportunities for overlapping runs can be set up during practice games and team scrimmages. Coaches should always alert the free fullback to such opportunities.

INTERCHANGE RUNS

Interchange runs differ from overlapping runs in that the players change position crossfield instead of downfield. For example, an inside forward would switch positions with his winger. As with overlapping runs, the objective in interchanging is to confuse the defense.

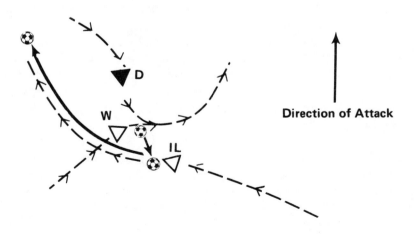

Figure 9. Interchange Run

In figure 9, a layoff pass from an attacking winger (W) to an inside left (IL) relieves pressure being applied by defender D. The defender's momentum in challenging the winger prevents him from recovering to challenge the inside left. The winger now runs in support on the inside, while the inside left makes a wing run with the ball.

Goalkeeper Tactics

An alert keeper can be just as much a playmaker as the full-backs playing in front of him. In fact, a keeper should serve as an extra fullback in addition to being a stopper of shots on goal. The reason many youngsters dislike playing keeper is their fear of missing the continuous action enjoyed by their team-mates. They certainly will be missing this action if they stay on their goal line and let the opponent strikers take potshots at them.

DEFENSIVE LATITUDE

By covering territory near the penalty area, an aggressive keeper can free the fullbacks to put more attacking pressure on the opposition. If the opposing team wins possession, the keeper has time to retreat behind the containment of the fullbacks. Also, a keeper can intercept balls passed behind the fullbacks, even outside the penalty area if necessary (remembering not to use his hands then).

A keeper's advanced position can also be useful if a fullback in possession of the ball receives a challenge. The fullback can turn the ball back to the keeper to relieve pressure and set up a counterattack. If a player in possession of the ball gets within range for a long shot, the keeper must retreat enough to prevent one being lobbed over his head.

The keeper should let his fullbacks know where he is while they have possession. A call of "keeper behind you" will let the ball carrier know he has support if he needs it. Once the keeper has called for the ball and it is sent to him, he must not hesitate to meet it—it could be intercepted if he does.

When the goalie gets the ball, he should waste no time serving it to a teammate. He should choose a teammate who is clear of immediate challengers. Many times, however, he will need to clear for distance. He should advance the ball to the top of the penalty area, dribbling it if necessary, before picking it up and clearing it. A very young keeper will have limited kicking range and should therefore clear the ball toward the wing on his side of the field—not down the middle and *never* across goal. Attackers are usually thickest in the middle and a weak clearance could be quickly turned against the out-of-position keeper.

GOALKEEPER/FULLBACK UNDERSTANDING

Good understanding must exist between a keeper and his fullbacks; otherwise, defensive errors occur that can give the opposition scoring chances. Common errors, all avoidable, are

1. Collisions between a fullback and the keeper when both try to intercept a long pass into the defense area. If the keeper decides to go for the ball, he must call for it, and the fullbacks must let him have it.

2. Passes back to the keeper finding their way into the net. Passes back to the keeper must always be made toward the areas on either side of the goal.

3. Short goal kicks being intercepted, either on the way to the receiver or afterward on the return to the keeper. The keeper decides whether a short or long goal kick is better; he should not take a short kick just because a fullback calls for the ball.

The fullbacks and keeper should function as a playing unit. This will require them to work out as many defensive understandings among themselves as they are mature enough to handle. Specific instruction from the coach in defensive plays will speed this process.

GOAL KICKS

A well-taken goal kick can set up a fast thrust into the opposition's territory. But a poorly-taken goal kick can set up a defensive nightmare. Coaches of inexperienced teams should have their best-kicking fullback take the goal kick and leave the keeper in the goalmouth. That will lessen the damage of a ball accidentally kicked to an attacker. If the keeper has the most talented kicking foot, he should take the goal kicks with a fullback guarding the goalmouth.

More mature, experienced teams, with no lack of kicking ability, may still fail to take advantage of the goal kick as an attacking tactic, using it just to get the ball back into play. It is worth trying to set up a fast shot on the opposition's goal if (1) the possession team looks for attacking space while the ball is being set up for the goal kick, and (2) the kicker selects the best placed receiver before setting up the ball, then gets the ball into play to that player quickly.

A good alternative to the long goal kick, particularly for short-kicking juniors, is the short goal kick (see fig. 10). Here, the keeper serves the ball to a fullback located just outside the penalty area. (Law XVI requires the ball to leave the penalty area to be in play.) The fullback LB then passes the ball back to the advancing keeper. The keeper should dribble the ball (if he picked it up immediately, he would be allowed only four steps before having to release it). At the head of the penalty area, the keeper picks up the ball and clears it to the advancing left half-back LH with a drop kick.

The advantage of this play is that the keeper can clear the ball much further with a drop kick from the top of the penalty

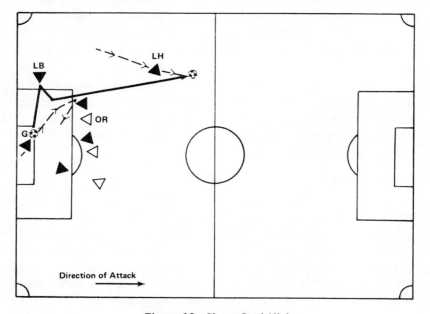

Figure 10. Short Goal Kick

area than with a deadball kick from the head of the goal area. However, an alert opponent (such as OR in fig. 10) could intercept the fullback's return pass to the keeper or place the receiving fullback under dangerous pressure. The keeper must decide whether or not a short goal kick should be taken, and it should be taken only if the receiving fullback is under no possible challenge pressure.

Group Tactics

Short-term objectives, such as the penetration of a defense, winning the ball, delaying progression of the ball while building an offense, or creating running space for a teammate carrying the ball may be achieved by two to four players working in tandem. The mechanics of group tactics are extensions of individual tactics. However, the understanding needed between participating players must be developed to a higher level since there are more decisions to be coordinated. And, team tactics start to be meaningful only when group tactical understanding begins to gel.

GROUP COMMUNICATION

Experienced team players know what their teammates tend to do in given tactical situations and can act accordingly without visual or audible signals. As skills advance further, predictability of teammate behavior is aided by recognition of body language. Knowing teammates' tendencies and being able to read their body language are the ultimate marks of a match-conditioned team. But team players acquire such ability only through sheer hard work, innumerable competitive matches, and demanding guidance from their coach.

Body language is the variety of physical attitudes a player assumes during play. An extreme example is immobility. A dribbler is discouraged from passing to an immobile supporting teammate. The idle teammate's attitude says, "If you pass to me, I am not ready to do anything with the ball." On the other hand, a dribbler serving a short, square pass is assured of a "walled" return pass not by calling for the ball, but by looking at the receiver and accelerating past the challenger. If the passer loses eye contact with the receiver or slows down as he passes the challenger, the receiver will probably keep the ball.

INTEGRATED PASSING

Close-support passing is generally thought of as a player serving the ball to an open, nearby teammate. Reverse that way of thinking and consider passing in terms of a nearby player working into an open position, then signaling for and receiving the ball.

The conventional way of thinking concentrates on coaching the server. The more comprehensive way of thinking encourages coaching the server and receiver as a unit, with the receiving player playing an active (if not dominant) role. This is how it must be if a team is going to achieve free-flowing, imaginative soccer. The receiver must accept responsibility for the passed ball and signal his teammate to serve to him. The receiver is in good position, is not under pressure, and has time to analyze the field array at the time. Therefore, the receiver is the best judge of whether the pass should be made to him or not. So, when a coach thinks of close-support passing in terms of receiver/server units, he will be well on his way to teaching a more positive, dynamic game.

Close-support passes fall into three basic categories: wall pass, double pass, and give-and-go. These passes find use mainly when striking under close marking from the opponent defense, but they can be used to beat a challenger anywhere on the field.

The passes characteristically proceed this way: the dribbler draws the challenger in close, touches the ball quickly to his supporting teammate, accelerates past the challenger, then collects a one-touch pass from the supporting teammate behind the challenger. The three basic passes are illustrated in figure 11.

The wall pass and double pass are similar in terms of technique and objective. However, the double pass includes an option. In the wall pass, the support player acts only as a "wall" for the dribbler to bounce the ball against. In the double pass, the support player positions himself so that he keeps the marking defender in sight; he then either splits the defense with a one-touch through pass to the dribbler, or he keeps the ball and maneuvers to pass the ball through outside the defender if the defender starts to cover the through pass space.

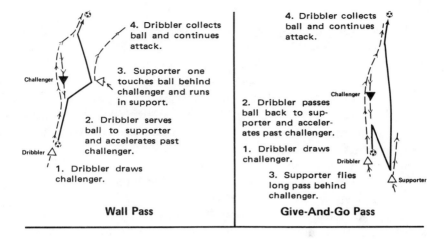

Wall Pass

4. Dribbler collects ball and continues attack.

3. Supporter one touches ball behind challenger and runs in support.

2. Dribbler serves ball to supporter and accelerates past challenger.

1. Dribbler draws challenger.

Give-And-Go Pass

4. Dribbler collects ball and continues attack.

2. Dribbler passes ball back to supporter and accelerates past challenger.

1. Dribbler draws challenger.

3. Supporter flies long pass behind challenger.

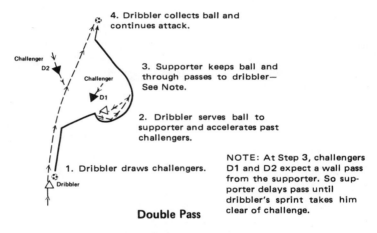

4. Dribbler collects ball and continues attack.

3. Supporter keeps ball and through passes to dribbler— See Note.

2. Dribbler serves ball to supporter and accelerates past challengers.

1. Dribbler draws challengers.

NOTE: At Step 3, challengers D1 and D2 expect a wall pass from the supporter. So supporter delays pass until dribbler's sprint takes him clear of challenge.

Double Pass

Figure 11. Close-Support Passes

DOUBLE-TEAMING

A coach's nightmare: the opposing team's superstar who single-handedly and continuously penetrates defenses without serious challenge. This calamity rarely happens, but it could, and a team must be prepared to handle it.

Challenging simultaneously with two defenders could be the answer. The tactic is called double-teaming. It is not the solution to shaky defensive play though, and before calling for double-teaming a coach should consider that the apparent superstar is just a capable dribbler made to look extra good by careless defensive work.

The fact is, double-teaming calls for more effort by the defense, not less, because an extra hole is opened up while two defenders are busy with one dribbler. The remaining defenders must share the added defensive responsibility.

The primary objective of double-teaming is to win the ball quickly, thus ending any chance of an effective offensive build-up. The secondary objective is to contain the dribbler and maneuver him to a part of the field where he is least dangerous —the corner area, touch line area, or his own half of the field. If neither of these objectives is fulfilled, the defense is left very porous and vulnerable to penetration.

A typical double-teaming play is shown in figure 12a. Challenge support is shown in figure 12b to illustrate the difference

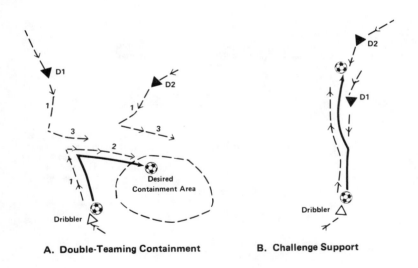

A. Double-Teaming Containment   B. Challenge Support

Figure 12. Defensive Two-on-One Tactics

between the two types of tactics. In the challenge support diagram, the defenders do not challenge simultaneously. Defender D2 challenges the dribbler only after the dribbler beats D1 and the ball gets a little ahead of the dribbler. (The superstar dribbler would not let the ball out of his control for a moment, so challenge support alone wouldn't get the job done.)

In the double-teaming diagram, the defenders have closed with the dribbler and have him under containment. They have positioned themselves so that, whichever way the dribbler tries to move, one of them can cut off his escape route. Under tightening pressure, the dribbler will eventually be forced into an error in judgment. At that time, the closest defender can tackle and win the ball.

If defender D1 in figure *a* forces the dribbler toward D2 and D2 relaxes his containment on the dribbler's right-hand side, the dribbler will be encouraged to move to his right. This is the essence of maneuvering a dribbler—making him think he has an escape route, allowing him to follow the escape route under tightly controlled cover, then reapplying the pressure when he arrives where the defenders want him.

In the double-teaming tactic, defenders must cooperate with a high level of understanding. This level is reached only if coaches drill their defensive players on this tactic during small-sided games.

NUMERICAL SUPERIORITY

One-on-one confrontations with opponents give no tactical advantage. There should always be one more player at the site of the ball than the opposition has. This tactic provides the dribbler on attack or the challenger on defense with the needed depth and width of field position to do his job.

The importance of width and depth is shown in figure 13.

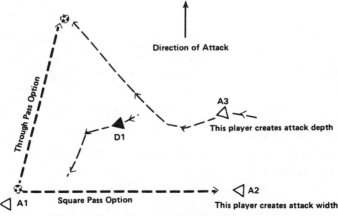

Figure 13. Importance of Width and Depth

Without the support of attacker A2, A1 could be forced into a duel with defender D1 because D1, with no worry about the attacking width provided by A2, could move to deny the attacking depth provided by A3. But with A2 present and D1 unsure of his defensive priorities (challenge A1 immediately or cover A2), A3 could sprint for the through pass when D1's attention is focused on A1 or A2.

The extra support player must be very careful to contribute to the play, rather than detract from it. He must be visible and available to his teammates if they need him. He must stay out of the way if they don't need him. For example, in figure 14a, attacker A2 has joined A1 and A3 in a three-on-two play against defenders D1 and D2. A3 is providing good attacking width and A2 is providing good attacking depth, if he is

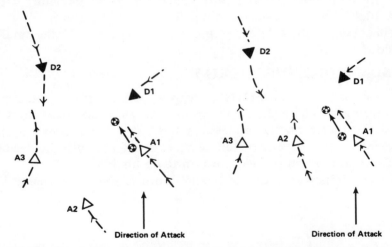

A. Effective numerical superiority—good width and depth of attack.

B. Ineffective numerical superiority— insufficient width and no depth of attack.

Figure 14. Numerical Superiority Advantage

needed. Now look at figure 14b. A2 has now moved between A1 and A3, destroying depth and reducing width. In fact, A3 is now in dead passing space and is probably not visible to dribbler A1. So, by ineffective use of the numerical superiority concept, A2 has destroyed the tactical advantage of the attacking team.

PATTERNED RUNS

The patterned run is the most demanding tactic in terms of teammate understanding. Players must be at the level where they can work together in evaluating the usefulness of space as it opens up on the field and turning it quickly into dribbling or passing space. Since the ball is in play, as contrasted to restart set-piece plays, the variations for patterned running are almost endless. The few examples described in this section should serve as a starting point for coaching patterned runs that suit the players' styles and capabilities.

The killer pass. Patterned runs are frequently set up to execute so-called "killer" passes, long through passes into the space behind the defense for a striker to sprint and collect. The timing of the striker's run and the serving of the pass must be synchronized; otherwise, the striker could be caught offside, or he might start his run early, thus signaling his intention to the defense.

A midfield killer pass is shown in figure 15. This type of play is typically executed by a linkman and an inside forward. To

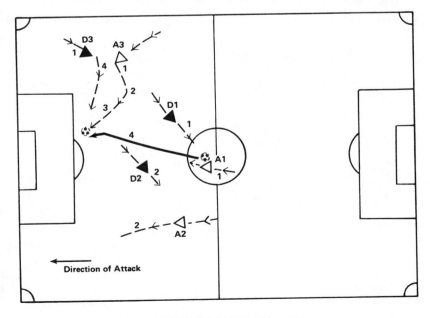

Figure 15. Midfield Killer Pass Play

execute it efficiently, the dribbler must have an obvious pass option and a "sleeper" pass option (that is, a pass option that is not obvious). In the example shown in figure 15, the play proceeds as follows:

1. Attacker A1 starts to draw defender D1 while A3 appears to soften pressure on D3. In turn, D3 will be encouraged to loosen his cover on A3.

2. A2 signals for a through pass, drawing D2 to the left side of the field to cover him.

3. A3, having lost the tight marking of D3 and having a slight midfield lead on him, sprints into the space behind D1 as D1 loses sight of A3.

4. Finally, A1 sends the killer pass for A3 to collect just before A3 goes beyond D3. (A1 must time his pass so that A3 does not go into offside position before the pass is served.)

A variation of the killer pass for wing plays is shown in figure 16. In this play, center forward A1 lays the ball back to wing half A2. A1 now decoys defenders D1 and D3 toward the center of the field. (D1 and D3 will be anticipating a return cross to

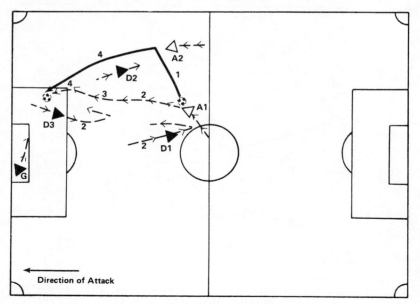

Figure 16. Wing Killer Pass Play

A1 from A2.) Meanwhile, A2 draws D2. With attacking space now opened up behind D2, A2 now serves the killer pass for A1 to run on, collect, and score.

Centering passes. Two different conditions exist on passes toward the goal from the wings. Each must be handled by its own kind of patterned run. As shown in figure 17a, a near-post cross is difficult to score from because of the narrow angle into goal available to receiver A2. A player in A4's position should always be available to receive a pass from the near-post receiver. Defenders such as D1 and the keeper will be moving toward A2 as the short-flighted pass is served by the winger, leaving a clear shot for A4.

The far-post cross leaves more shooting chances, as shown in figure 17b. If the pass is low enough across the goalmouth, the

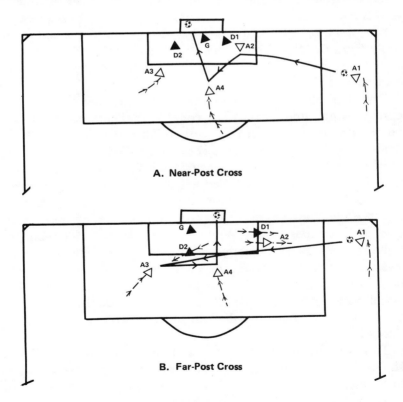

A. Near-Post Cross

B. Far-Post Cross

Figure 17. Cross-Goal Patterns

inside forwards could have a chance with a head shot. But the most productive far-post cross is flighted so that it swerves toward the head of an approaching player on the opposite wing.

As shown in figure 17b, A3 has deflected the ball to A4 for a clear shot on goal. Had the keeper not covered A3, A3 could have headed the ball directly into goal. Since there is little time under pressure for A3 to determine whether or not A4 is running into position to receive a pass, A4 must always run a pattern as shown to be either available for the pass or to draw the attention of the keeper away from A3.

RESTARTS

Soccer is one of the most unstructured of all team games. The play is so dynamic and fluid that preplanning of tactics is rarely possible at the basic level of youth soccer. Even advanced youths can be coached in only a limited number of set pieces.

But planning can be done to get the ball into play productively from deadball conditions. The restarts described in this section are easy to execute and can be elaborated on by the creative coach.

Training for set pieces consists solely of setting up and executing restarts under rehearsed conditions. Therefore, there are no training references in this section. The set pieces should be drilled regularly. Those set pieces that failed during the last match should always be restaged at the following practice session to find out why they failed and how to remedy the failure.

Kickoff. At kickoff time, inside forwards have a big responsibility. They have to choose between several passing options, or elect to keep possession. At that time, there is no offensive buildup, and eager challengers are no more than ten yards away. If the inside forwards elect to keep possession, they will be under immediate pressure and could easily lose the ball. The better option is to buy time to create an offensive buildup. (The offensive buildup is described in chapter 4 under "Offensive Tactics.")

Time can be bought with the kickoff tactic shown in figure 18. Attacker A1 kicks off to A2, who immediately passes back to A3 (usually the center half). The defending team cannot challenge immediately and the resulting delay allows A3 to select passing options. The wingers will usually have progressed downfield and, if they have done their job properly, will have found space in which to receive a penetrating pass, as has A4 in figure 18.

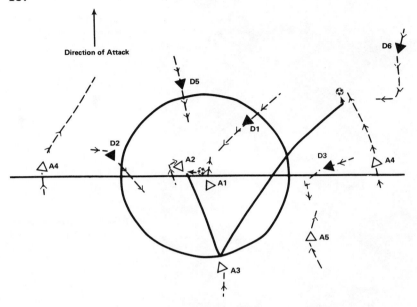

Figure 18. Kickoff Delay Tactic

Throw-in. The throw-in could be treated as just another pass situation, except for one important difference: the opposition has a chance to set up a defense against the pass during collection of the out-ball. Defensive pressure may be light if the ball is not in the attack zone, but a smart defense will close in on any open receivers if the point of throw-in is close to their goal. However, with simple signals and a speedy restart, an effective attack can be started in spite of tight marking.

An example of hand signals is shown in figure 19. The receiver uses his hand, out of the defending player's sight, to signal that he wants the ball thrown in to his right. He then fakes sharply to his left, throwing the defender's balance in that direction. With the defender's momentum going to his left, the player throwing in the ball now throws the ball in to the receiver's right and the receiver sprints to collect it unchallenged. Similar variations can be made for a throw-in to the left (right hand pointing left) or a throw-in over the defender's head

A. Signal for ball to be thrown to receiver's right.

B. Fake to put marking defender off-balance to his left.

C. Throw in to the receiver's right.

Figure 19. Throw in Signaling

(thumb pointing upward). In this last case, the fake of the receiver would be toward the player throwing in to draw the defender forward.

Corner kicks. A player's choice of long or short corner kicks will be decided largely by age and experience. Very junior teams (say, seven to twelve years old) will usually not have the kicking power to fly the ball into or beyond the goalmouth. So, for this age group, the short corner kick is advisable.

Older youths may have the power to send the ball to the center of the goalmouth or beyond to the far post. But without well-drilled set-piece plans, the challenge for the ball becomes a pandemonium instead of a smoothly executed strike.

With the large numbers of defensive and offensive players involved in a corner kick, the variety of set-piece plays for corner kicks is large. It would not be practical to try coaching them all. A few basic plays that are practical for a team's capabilities should allow the team to be effective against any kind of defense. Considerations for long and short corner kicks vary; a coach has to decide player assignments and play patterns after much experimentation.

Figure 20a shows a long corner kick flighted to drop into the center of the goalmouth (in this illustration, only the key players are shown). Ideally, the inside forwards should act as decoys to clear defenders from the goalmouth. This leaves the center forward or center half to run onto the ball for a clear head shot on goal. He runs from an unmarked position as the ball is curving outward to meet his head. The outswerving ball will be going away from the defenders, making it difficult to clear. It will be going toward the striker, making it easy to connect with and providing additional impact speed.

A ball flighted beyond goal center probably will not require decoying the defense away from it. A winger moving in on a timed run will be able to meet the ball high and head it into goal without challenge.

Near-post crosses are not usually suitable for head or volley shots. Except for very skillful youngsters, the angle into goal for a head or volley shot is too narrow. A more productive move is for the pass target to meet a ground pass from the corner kicker, as shown in figure 20b, then serve the ball to the approaching corner kicker for a direct shot on goal. This tactic is a varia-

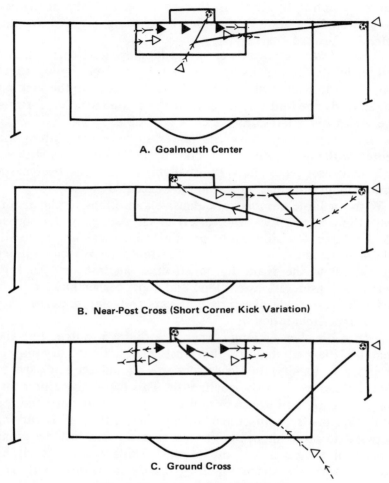

A. Goalmouth Center

B. Near-Post Cross (Short Corner Kick Variation)

C. Ground Cross

Figure 20. Corner Kick Variations

tion of the short-corner kick.

A similar play to the near-post short corner kick is the "short short" corner. A midfielder approaches the corner down the wing and receives a short pass from the corner kicker. The midfielder then shoots directly on goal or maneuvers the ball for a closer shot. (He must be careful not to pass while any teammate is in offside position.)

A ground cross is shown in figure 20c. The decoy responsibility of the inside forwards is the same as in the goalmouth center; that is, to clear the defense from the goalmouth. On a timed run from an unmarked position, the wing halfback (typically) can take a direct shot on goal from just inside the penalty area.

Free kick. Set-piece planning for free kicks gives a coach a showcase for his creative talents. Intelligent assignment of player duties and frequent drilling of free-kick restarts will produce healthy scoring opportunities from anywhere in the attack zone. For free-kick restarts outside the attack zone, it is more productive to make a short pass and start an offensive buildup than to fly the ball long into the middle of the attack zone (unless the defense is obviously disorganized).

The key ingredient to successful free-kick restarts is speed. Often, the opposing team is busy arguing with the referee or trying to find out why the game is stopped. The fouled team does not have to wait for a restart whistle unless the referee has signaled for the team to wait (for example, he will signal the team to wait if he has to move opponents back to their 10-yard limit from the ball). So, a coach should train his team to restart as soon as possible after the foul has been called, to catch the opposing team without an organized defense.

The only planning needed for penalty kicks is the assignment of a trustworthy shooter. In practices, statistics should be kept on how consistently each player can place the ball in a given corner of the goal. Avoid making a permanent assignment on the basis of a few drills and do not try forwards only; the sharpshooter of the team could be a fullback.

The usual defenses against free kicks in the attack zone are a player wall (fig. 21) for direct free kicks and close marking of all potential receivers for indirect free kicks. If the opposing team has had a chance to set up these defenses, a few basic methods of beating them are available, with dozens of creative variations.

To beat a wall, a shooter must put the ball over it, around it, or through it. His choice will depend on several factors: how far the wall is from the goal, how well the wall is covering the goal, how tight the wall is, and how teammates and opponents are positioned outside the wall.

If the wall is far enough from the goal, the shooter could possibly send the ball over the wall and under the crossbar, giving

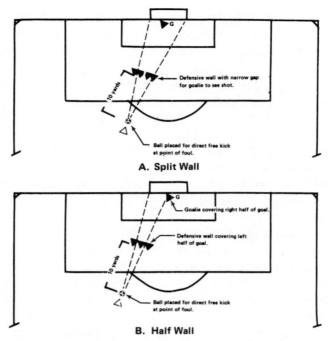

A. Split Wall

B. Half Wall

Figure 21. Setting up Wall for Direct Free Kick Defense

the ball sufficient top spin to make it rise and then drop sharply. If the ends of the wall do not overlap the line of sight to the goal posts by too great a margin, the shooter could bend the ball around the wall and find the inside of the goal posts. But these options call for good ball skills and, unless the team has a shooter of this caliber, scoring chances are slight.

A more reliable option is penetrating the wall. It is sometimes possible to imbed attacking players in a defensive wall and have them leave the wall as the ball is kicked, thus leaving an opening for a direct shot on goal. If the shooter misses the hole and hits the wall, the teammates may still have a shot with the rebound.

Sometimes it is wiser to select an indirect approach, even though a direct free kick has been awarded. For instance, when facing a well-organized, tightly-knit defensive wall, a carefully taken indirect free kick, using a "peel off" tactic, could pay dividends. In this play, two supporting players jam themselves against the ends of the wall, taking care to remain slightly forward of the wall so they are not in offside position. The kicker passes the ball outside the wall, one of the end players peels off, catches the ball before a defender does, and shoots on goal.

The wall peel-off technique is shown in figure 22. The weight (speed) of the pass and the playacting of the attackers are critical. The weight of the pass must be enough to surprise the defenders in the wall, but slow enough to allow A3 to collect it instead of an alert keeper. The playacting of the attackers must keep the defenders guessing which end of the wall is going to receive the ball. Getting the defenders to commit against a pass faked to A2 leaves A3 free to collect the actual pass and score.

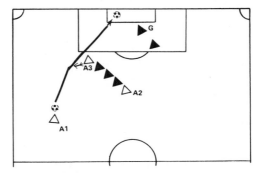

Figure 22. Wall Peel-Off Tactic for Free Kicks

OFFSIDE TRAP

The offside trap is a timed movement by a defensive player or, more usually, a group of defensive players working as a unit. The tactic puts a deep attacker in offside position *just before* his teammate passes the ball towards him. A server downfield will not usually be able to tell that his receiver has just been put in offside position.

In the play shown in figure 23, defender D1, who is marking attacker A1, anticipates the pass from A3 to A1. D1 sets the trap by maneuvering to A1's blind side and then moving further from the goal line than A1 (move 1). A1, who is watching for the pass, fails to notice. Now A1 is in offside position because he has only one opponent, the keeper, between him and the goal line. A1 is not guilty of an offside infraction yet because the ball has not been passed toward him; that is, the trap has only been set, not sprung. The instant A3 passes the ball toward

A1 (move 2), D1's offside trap will be sprung and up will go the linesman's flag.

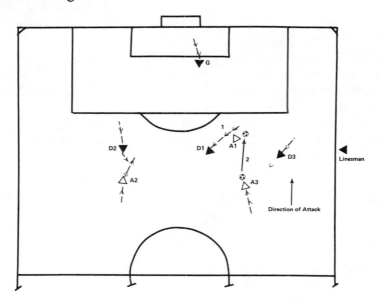

1. D1 puts A1 in offside position just before A3 releases ball to A1. (No infraction yet.)

2. A3 releases ball to A1. Linesman immediately signals offside infraction on A1.

Figure 23. Offside Trap

A coach must make defenders aware of two dangers in this elegant tactic:

1. If the officials miss the offside infraction, A1 will be rewarded with a one-on-one duel with the keeper.

2. An unaware defenseman (D2 or D3 in fig. 23) could fall back before the ball is released to A1, putting A1 onside again with a good lead downfield on D1.

This tactic can be a source of continual frustration to high-pressure strikers. To be able to use the offside trap, however, a team must have confidence in the officials, they must understand the offside rule, and they must be sufficiently coordinated to make it work. The play should be taught only when the coach feels his players can concentrate on more than the immediate needs of one-on-one challenges for the ball.

Team Tactics

Team tactics imply continuous coordinated activity by eleven players to achieve a tactical objective. Just as in individual and group tactics, there is never a good reason for players to be idle, regardless of which team has the ball (or even whether the ball is in or out of play). Nevertheless, inexperienced players often stand immobile when not close to the ball. Continuity of play for all players on a team is imperative—the game does not end for players when the ball moves a few yards away from them.

OFFENSIVE AND DEFENSIVE MODES

To carry the concept of play continuity one step further, consider another important tactical concept: total soccer. This concept generally means throwing out "classical" tactical defensive and offensive player assignments and letting each team member do what is necessary at the time to get the job done. The concept requires all team members to be expert at their own jobs, and be thoroughly familiar with each others' methods of play.

At basic levels, coaching total soccer is not practical because the players are not equipped to handle such decison-making and skill requirements. However, one useful idea for inexperienced players can be borrowed from total soccer: If a team is in possession of the ball, *all* team members are in an offensive mode. On the other hand, if a team is not in possession of the ball, *all* team members are in a defensive mode. Chaos results when some players employ defensive tactics while the rest of the team is on the attack, or employ offensive tactics while the rest are on defense.

A coach shouldn't talk to his players in exactly those terms. Should he, he might find his inexperienced players crowding their own teammate in possession of the ball; or, they will all jam themselves into their own goalmouth when an opposing player gets possession of the ball. But teaching inexperienced players to think offensively when their teammate has the ball will encourage them to be alert for good scoring chances. Teaching them to think defensively when an opponent has the ball will encourage them to cover scoring threats on their own goal more closely.

TEAM MOBILITY

The general kickoff pattern of the system must be maintained during play; otherwise, players start to bunch up. The entire team, in unit formation (forwards, halfbacks, and fullbacks), should move up and down the field as the ball moves up and down the field. To a lesser extent, they should also move across the field as the ball works from one side to the other. This general team movement with the ball is termed "compactness" of play. If this coordinated mobility does not happen, large spaces open up on the field and destroy effective offensive teamwork. Such spaces hurt defensive play by giving the opposing team room for advancing the ball rapidly without challenge.

The preceding is an oversimplified picture of the dynamics of a soccer game. However, it does illustrate the need to teach inexperienced players positional soccer. As their tactical awareness improves, they will be able to handle more flexible positional assignments.

One of the most difficult positional problems a coach has to deal with in very young players is "swarming" around the ball in play like bees around a jelly jar. Their enthusiasm to be a part of the action puts all thoughts of positional play out of their minds. The root of this problem is usually immobility of the dribbler; the ball has come to a standstill and is attracting players from both teams. A ball kept in motion by dribbling or passing never has the chance to be the center of a swarm.

Immobility is usually caused by lack of ball skills. The ball receiver cannot get the ball under control and moving before the swarm descends on him. Or, he freezes under challenge and gets swarmed. Or, he miskicks it just a few feet when trying to pass to a teammate, and again that same pesky swarm descends on him.

No tactical drills will remedy a lack of ball skills. But once these swarming youngsters gain sufficient skills to give them time to look around under pressure, tactical training such as scrimmages with touch restriction (described in chapter 6) will clear up swarming problems.

4

Game Dynamics

This chapter puts individual, group, and team tactics into the working environment of the soccer match. For ninety minutes, the big picture is game tactics: offensive and defensive. The personnel tactics described so far form the threads that bind the fabric of game tactics together.

Offensive Tactics

Offensive tactics can be thought of as having four sequences: acquisition and retention of the ball, offensive buildup, penetration of the defense, and the strike. Acquisition of the ball ends a team's defensive mode—all members of the team should start thinking in terms of offense.

The offensive buildup sequence consists of improvising plays that allow players time to position themselves for defense penetration. During defense penetration, the ball carrier and supporting players try to open up (split) the defense to get the ball within striking range. The strike is the final play, the one that puts the ball in the back of the net.

OFFENSIVE BUILDUP

If a player (say, a midfielder) acquires the ball in his own half of the field, he may not have forwards downfield to pass to. He must then work the ball himself or coordinate play with his immediate support to gain buildup time. This is called improvisation.

While the midfield players are improvising, the forwards should look for defensive weaknesses and position themselves where they can exploit those weaknesses. Meanwhile, the midfielders will work themselves into supporting offensive positions (see fig. 24).

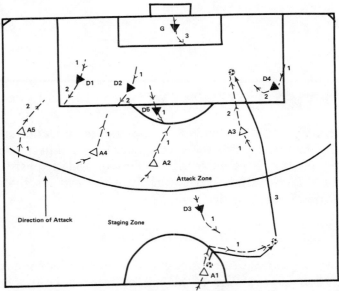

1. Attacker A1 draws defender D3 from defensive concentration and delays ball penetration as A2, A3, and A4 deploy offensively.

2. A3 sprints for space as D4 overcommits on defense.

3. A1 flies ball into space in back of D4 for A3 to collect and strike.

Figure 24. Offensive Buildup

The improvisation activity will take place in the preparation (or staging) zone, which is the middle third of the field. It is the area from which the final attack on goal is launched. (It is also the area in which the defensive buildup is initiated.)

A sudden pass from the ball carrier to one of the forwards or attacking midfielders will put immediate pressure on the defense. With the ball deep in the defenders' third of the field, the offensive fullbacks can move to or beyond midfield to intensify pressure. It makes for a pressure-cooker effect: the forwards turn on the heat, the midfielders put the lid on, and the fullbacks clamp down the lid.

If an attacking player acquires the ball in the attack zone through a quick counterattack and the defense is disorganized, a buildup (built offense) may not be needed. Penetration could be achieved through solo improvisation by the player who acquired the ball. At most, one other teammate might participate.

There is no telling where or when the ball may be acquired or how effectively the defense will get organized once it is. To increase scoring chances following turnovers, especially those at midfield, a team should keep one forward, possibly two, in a deep forward position at all times. This can be done without weakening the defense. The deep forwards, who stay just short of being offside, present a continuous threat. Deep forwards on defense discourage opposing fullbacks from advancing too far in support of their own forwards. And, if possession is gained, deep forwards represent the potential for a surprise strike, or, once midfield support builds up behind them, for a concentrated assault on goal. They also provide a "relief valve" for the defense; without them, a cleared ball would be returned without challenge.

The deployment of midfielders and forwards shortly after the ball is won can spell the difference between success and failure. Deployment is described in terms of width and depth. An example of a deep offensive pattern is shown in figure 25a. The eight players involved lead or lag each other substantially and are aligned generally down the center of the field. The support

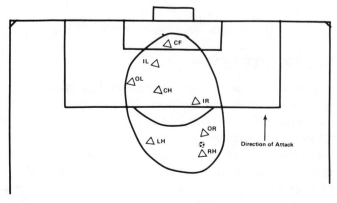

Figure 25a. Deep Offense

consists mainly of through passes. Buildup is fast and direct:
however, the pattern is relatively easy to defend against because
the narrow paths available for the through passes make interception easy.

A wide, or flat, offensive pattern is shown in figure 25b. The
players span the field. The support consists mainly of square
passes; therefore, the buildup will be slower and less direct.
Unlike the deep buildup, it is hard to defend against because of
the wide openings available to the square passer.

The most effective buildup is a balanced one, that is, one that
employs both deep and wide patterns of attack. A combination
of laterally and vertically deployed players ensures possession of
the ball while making a direct assault on goal.

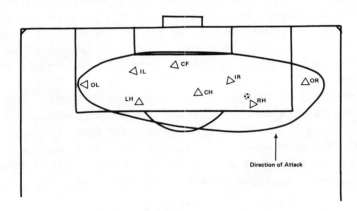

Figure 25b. Wide (Flat) Offense

DEFENSE PENETRATION

The more confrontations a ball carrier has with opponents,
the slower his progress and the fewer his penetration chances. If
he is a capable dribbler, but has no support and only one defender to beat, he must be prepared to beat the challenger one-
on-one. However, when faced with several defenders, he must
either beat them all or avoid challenge until help arrives. Avoid-
ing challenge is more likely to pay off. All that is needed is
some friendly running space in which to hide until that help
arrives.

The ball carrier can make running space for himself or an

overlapping teammate by sheer fakery. Even players who are not immediately responsible for defense (that is, those furthest from the ball) tend to move toward the ball carrier. So, by dribbling the ball toward a fake target area, the ball carrier can entice the defense out of good cover position (see fig. 26). Then, he can either accelerate into the opened running space or send the ball to a teammate overlapping down the now weakened side of the field.

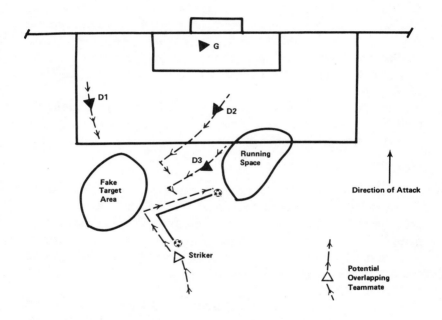

Figure 26. Patterned Run Dribbling

The ball carrier, if he is very successful in this kind of patterned run, could even make penetration space for himself and go through for a strike unaided. However, he will usually need some decoy help (refer to chapter 3 under "Decoy Runs") in making openings in the defense. At less advanced levels, a coach should develop the close-support passing skills of his team to open up penetration chances (refer to chapter 3 under "Close Support Passes").

STRIKING

The more skillful the penetration, the better the chances of executing an unpressured shot on goal. But such chances are rarely given away by a determined, well-coached defense. So, when the time comes for striking (sometimes called "finishing"), the offensive team should take any halfway reasonable scoring chances that present themselves. The surprise element in striking is all-important. The long shot through a crowded defense pays off frequently in own-goals (shots that deflect off a defender into his own goal). The crudely struck shot taken off-balance sometimes catches even the most experienced goalies unprepared to handle the spin on the ball. And the "trash" goal scored from a goalpost rebound or goalie's fumble counts every bit as much as the carefully planned and executed "classical" shot.

Once players know their strike capabilities, they should not hesitate to shoot the first time chances present themselves— they may not get second chances.

OFFSIDE AVOIDANCE

In their eagerness to score, even experienced players wander into offside position. Inexperienced players stray to an offside position simply because they are not familiar with the offside rules. Even once they are familiar with the rules, players will go into an offside position because they are concentrating only on the activity around the ball, and not paying attention to the defenders as well.

First, all players must understand Law XI (the offside rules). Not only forwards must know these rules, but defenders must know them so that they are able to plan and execute offside traps (described in chapter 3).

Second, the defense is not likely to be standing still. Therefore, players in position to strike must watch the ball *and* the rearmost defender no matter where they go (fig. 27).

Defensive Tactics

There are also four parts to defensive tactics: loss of the ball, chase and delay, defensive buildup, and challenge. On loss of possession all team members should respond defensively. The

A. Fullback on blind side of attacker, about to put attacker in offside position.

Figure 27. Offside Avoidance

chase-and-delay sequence denies the ball carrier running space while the defensive buildup is put into effect. The defensive buildup sequence is a covering and marking action; its goal is to place defenders in positions where all threats from attackers can be covered. The challenge is that portion of defensive tactics in which the defending team attempts to win the ball.

CHASE AND DELAY

Tactics for the chase and delay vary depending on where possession was lost. In the worst possible case, where possession is lost in a team's own goalmouth, there is no time to execute a chase-and-delay sequence, let alone a defensive buildup. Immediate challenge is a must. On the other hand, if possession is lost deep in the opponent's territory, the ball carrier can be delayed while a defensive buildup is executed in an orderly way. Then, when the challenge sequence is started, there will be maximum pressure on the ball carrier because all his passing options are denied him.

The defender closest to the attacking ball carrier is the obvious choice as the ball carrier's opponent. His delaying tactic is containment; that is, staying in front of the dribbler and denying him dribbling space. While containing the dribbler, he should try to maneuver him toward the outside of the field. This way, if the ball carrier does manage to beat the challenger, the ball carrier has further to go toward the more dangerous central part of the field. If the challenger is having difficulty containing the ball carrier, he should work in coordination with another defender to double-team the ball carrier, as described in chapter 3 under "Double-Teaming."

DEFENSIVE BUILDUP

Important priorities must be observed in the defensive build-up. Defensive support players must cover and mark opponents to put the opposing ball carrier under pressure by cutting off his pass targets. In covering, the defending player places himself between his own goal and a potential pass target so that he can quickly challenge if the pass target receives the ball. In marking, a defensive player places himself alongside a potential pass target, threatening to intercept any pass his way. In figure 28, defender D2 has committed the serious, but common, error of ball watching. By losing sight of attacker A4, D2 has allowed a through pass from A1 to drop into the space where D2 should

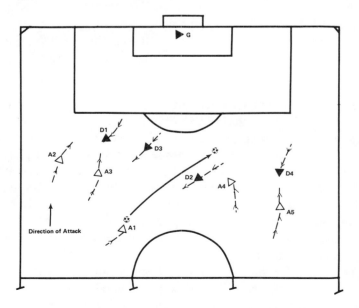

Figure 28. Defensive Covering Error

have been (point X). A4 is rewarded with an unchallenged strike on goal.

As the ball approaches the goal, the defenders should start closing the distance between themselves and the opponents they have been covering. When the ball reaches the penalty area, all potential pass targets should be marked, not just covered. Then the ball carrier, having no passing options, is forced into a one-on-one confrontation with a challenger.

To stay between the attackers and their own goal, defenders must retreat as the attacking team advances. This retreating action is called "funneling back" (fig. 29), because the effective playing area tends to decrease to a narrow "neck" of defensive concentration as the ball approaches the defense zone (striking zone for the attackers).

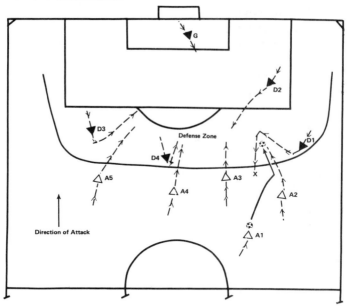

Point X is ideal point of tackle for D1. All attackers nearing defense zone are marked. D2 is providing challenge support for D1 while marking A3.

Figure 29. Defensive Buildup

Width and depth are as important a consideration for the defensive buildup as the offensive. The deep defensive array shown in figure 30a slows up penetration down the center of the

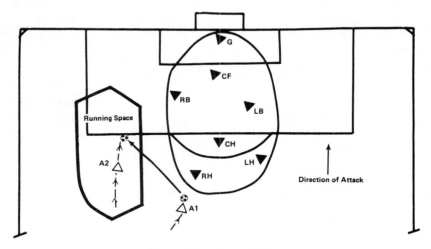

Figure 30a. Deep Defense

field but leaves the wings open for penetration. The flat defensive array shown in figure 30b makes penetration a danger across the width of the field. If ball carrier A1 beats opposing halfback LH, he beats all of the opposing halfbacks and has running space behind them. All he has to do then is beat the opposing left fullback and he is one-on-one with the keeper. Or, he can fly the ball into the space behind the fullbacks for A2 to collect and strike.

Again, the key is balance—to cover the field in such a way that all challengers have backup support but with no gaps left that can be easily exploited with through passes.

CHALLENGING

Ideally, the first direct challenge to win the ball should be made before the attackers cross into the striking area. This way, the defending team will have a chance to win the ball before a serious scoring threat develops.

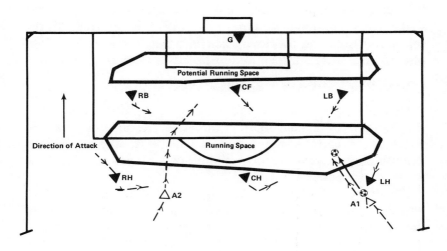

Figure 30b. Wide (Flat) Defense

The other extreme—the far-from-ideal situation in which possession is lost in the goalmouth—may find the goalkeeper out of position and several attackers unmarked. The defensive plan calls for swift, cool action. A coach cannot practice this situation enough. Strict action priorities must be observed as follows:

1. The defender closest to the striker moves in front of, and in tight to, the striker. This way, the striker cannot get off a clear shot on goal. The containing defender stays in this position, no matter where the striker moves.

2. The goalkeeper positions himself in relation to the movements of the ball. At the same time, the immediate defenders tightly mark all attackers in the defense zone.

3. A backup defender positions himself behind the containing defender. (If the action is very close to the goal, the backup defender may well be the goalkeeper.)

4. The containing defender tackles for possession of the ball.

(If the containing defender tackles earlier than step 3, the striker may beat him and have a clear shot on goal. If the containing defender tackles earlier than step 2, the striker could pass to an unmarked teammate who has a clear shot on goal.)

CONSTRUCTIVE OR DESTRUCTIVE DEFENSE

Defensive play can be and should be exciting. Some say the buildup of a goal-scoring threat is the exciting part to watch. To a certain extent that is true. But, without a keen defense there could be no buildup of excitement. Suspense builds excitement.

The defense should think in terms of playmaking rather than play destroying. A coach should encourage his team to think of the defensive sequences as preliminaries to counterattacks. Players who think of defense as nothing more than plays to stop scoring threats will spend their time as play destroyers.

Play-destroying leads to dull soccer. For example, it is frustrating to watch a defender kick the ball over the touchline in panic when just a few yards away stands an open teammate who could start a counterattack. The panicky defender has turned the ball over to the opposing team, placing his team on the defensive again. Kicking the ball out of touch should be the last resort; that is, it should be done only when the goal is in immediate danger and there is insufficient support to prevent a shot on goal or to initiate a counterattack.

The Importance of Pressure in Tactics

Pressure is to soccer what emotion is to romance: it would work without it but who would care? Pressure enables a match-fit team to beat a technically superior but less energetic team. Continuous harassment can prevent the better team from using its skills effectively. Then, frustration, discouragement, and fatigue will cause the downfall of the less energetic team.

Youngsters, particularly preteenagers, are heavily influenced by pressure. In fact, the pressure of being one goal behind early in a game is enough to make some youngsters give up. Older, more game-wise youths, on the other hand, are often spurred on to greater efforts by this same pressure.

A team that looks great one week and bad the next is a team

that has not yet matured. It cannot handle match pressures. Any team looks only as good as its opponents allow.

PRESSURE IN INDIVIDUAL TACTICS

Pressure is the key ingredient in challenging and containing, double-teaming, decoy running, and other one-on-one or two-on-one play. Pressure makes a dribbler give the ball up to a challenger, it maneuvers a dribbler into unrewarding space, or it makes a defender follow the decoy run of a seemingly dangerous off-the-ball attacker.

PRESSURE IN GROUP TACTICS

Pressure in defensive group tactics allows a unit of defenders to break up a strike on goal by tight marking of all attackers. In offensive tactics, a wing/wing-half attacking combination can pressure an entire defensive unit out of position to leave running room for their winger on the opposite side of the field to collect a crossfield pass.

This kind of wide-open game pressure can be executed only by older youths. Preteens, having only limited kicking power, have to play a more "local" game; however, while they cannot put field-switching pressure on their opponents, they can switch play quickly to the opposite perimeter of play when it is weakly defended.

PRESSURE IN TEAM TACTICS

Team tactics can be characterized as either low or high pressure. In low pressure tactics, emphasis is on careful buildup of superior field position and reacting to the opponents' moves. In high pressure tactics, defenses are man-to-man rather than zone (that is, a defender always covers an opponent, rather than an area on the field), and offenses are mounted by counterattacks as soon as the ball is won.

It is interesting to note that teams using high-pressure defensive tactics usually adopt low-pressure offensive tactics. The reverse is true of teams using low-pressure defensive tactics; they usually employ high-pressure offensive tactics on counterattack. The dynamics of pressure in offensive and defensive tactics generally run as follows:

High-Pressure Defense

1. Man-to-man marking assignments; that is, each player is assigned to mark a counterpart on the opposing team.

2. Two-on-one duels with the ball carrier (see chapter 3 under "Numerical Superiority").

3. All attackers closely marked, no matter where the ball is.

4. Minimal defensive buildup. Maximum effort is applied to regain the ball as soon as possible after losing it.

Low-Pressure Defense

1. Zone coverage by defenders.

2. One-on-one containment of the ball carrier.

3. Careful coverage of opponents, but no marking until the ball has been advanced to the defense zone.

4. Maximum defense buildup. Challenge support is mandatory before tackling for possession of the ball.

Low-Pressure Offense

1. Forwards rely on close support from their midfielders rather than be improvisers themselves.

2. Slow offensive buildup, with delaying improvisation at midfield.

3. Frequent interchange plays designed to disorganize the defense (see chapter 3 under "Interchange Runs").

4. Usually practiced by teams using a high-pressure defense. This is because successful high-pressure defense (fast recovery of the ball after losing it) leaves the opponent fullbacks and midfielders still relatively organized and capable of defending against a fast, unsupported counterattack.

High-Pressure Offense

1. One or more forwards always in the attack zone, or as far forward as possible without being in offside position.

2. Frequent overlapping runs (see chapter 3 under "Overlapping and Recovery Runs").

3. Fast counterattacks by long through passes.

4. Usually practiced by teams using a low-pressure defense. This is because low-pressure defensive tactics—for example,

funneling back—draw the opponent fullbacks and midfielders deep downfield, leaving them disorganized and vulnerable to a fast counterattack.

An example of high-pressure offense is shown in figure 31 (only a few key players are shown to avoid clutter). Team B (except for their center forward) has funneled back, organizing a low-pressure defense against team A. The team A fullbacks and midfielders are moving up close behind the ball carrier (the team A right halfback) to pressurize team B.

The team B left halfback forces the ball carrier to make a bad pass, which is intercepted by the team B center halfback. The center halfback quickly flies the ball to the center forward, who is free of the disorganized team A defense and in good field position for a fast strike on goal.

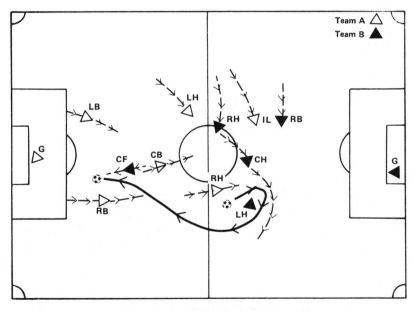

Figure 31. Example of a Low-Pressure Defense Developing into a High-Pressure Offense

5

Match Analysis

There are drills for remedying any skill weaknesses conceivable. Such training is covered in chapter 6. But careful match analysis is required for a coach to determine which skills are deficient and which remedial practices are necessary.

Match analysis is a method for considering all team contributions to any given match situation and determining if these contributions are positive or negative. The idea is to identify the source of whatever problem a team is experiencing. There may be several problems involved, and they must be isolated and dealt with one by one. Attempts to solve several problems with the same remedy are inefficient and can lead to additional problems.

Analytical Thinking

Figure 32 outlines a coach's thought process as he analyzes a typical match problem—in this case, lack of scoring power. This approach can be used to isolate any match-related problem, whether it is a tactical, physical, or technique deficiency. The experienced coach goes through this type of process automatically for several different situations in each match.

This system will help prevent rash judgments. For instance, a hasty appraisal of a scoring problem may lead a coach to

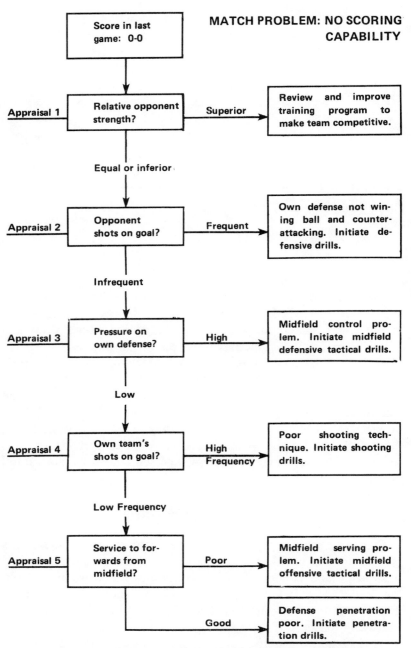

Figure 32. Simplified Thought Processes in Match Analysis

assume the trouble is in his forward line. After all, which unit has the major responsibility for scoring? But, if the forwards cannot get service from behind, the team is going to lack scoring punch. Or, if a team's defense is always bottled up, the forwards are always going to be pressed into defensive service, which is not the most productive thing for forwards to be doing.

APPRAISING THE PROBLEM

In figure 32, the coach examines his team and the opposition from the forwards to the keeper. Assume he judged the opposition inferior (appraisal 1): the game result should have been a win for his team. Had the opposition been superior, he could have lived with a scoreless tie and decided to bring his team up to par over the length of the season.

If the opponents outshot his team (Appraisal 2), chances are his defense is not able to win the ball and feed it forward. On the other hand, if they did not outshoot his team, he must decide whether it was due to effective fullbacking or tight midfield control (Appraisal 3). If pressure on the fullbacks was high, yet shots on goal were infrequent, the fullbacks were working effectively but midfield control was being lost by the halfbacks. If pressure on the fullbacks was low, the midfielders were in defensive control. The blame appears to lie with either the forwards or the midfielders in their servicing support.

If the team had managed many shots on goal (Appraisal 4), then support from midfield and penetration were likely adequate. Frequent penetration that produces infrequent scoring usually indicates a lack of shooting talent on the part of the strikers.

When the forwards manage few shots on goal, the coach must determine whether or not they were getting possession of the ball (Appraisal 5). If the midfield was not serving the ball through, midfield offensive drills should be initiated. However, if service to the forwards was adequate, the trouble lies with the forwards' inability to penetrate the defense.

RESOLVING THE PROBLEM

Now, the coach must decide what are the elements of the problem, the problem in this sample case being lack of defense-penetration capability. Defense penetration requires high-speed dribbling under pressure, accurate, one-touch passing, and decoy runs. So the practice session can be designed to improve defense penetration like this:

1. Warmups: Give-and-go passing drills while running as a group under one-touch restriction (see chapter 6 under "Drill Restrictions").

2. Technique Training: Drill forwards and midfielders in high-speed dribbling runs with one-touch support partners. The last return pass to the striker should be laid on properly for a first-time shot on goal.

3. Tactical Training: Use offensive small-sided games (up to four-on-three), then scrimmage the team. Place the same conditions on them that were imposed during the small-sided games; for example, the dribbler must beat one defender before passing, or the dribbler must pass and sprint for a return pass.

Such programming takes a team from warmups through tactical training, orienting everything toward defense penetration. It is pure objective coaching.

6

Tactical Training

Training boils down to a lot of hard work for both coaches and players. A coach must not let this hard work go to waste; his players must leave their mistakes on the practice field and take their accomplishments onto the competition pitch. How can a coach see that they do? By careful analysis of their match performance, application of progressive training principles, and remedial training to strengthen their game in the specific areas needed.

Progressive Training Principles

The training program should progress as follows in each of the areas of concern to the coach.

Fitness: Increasing intensity of activity, more repetitions of a given activity, and reducing rest intervals between activities.

Technique: Mastering ball skills under increasing pressure (from none up to match pressure). All skill drills should end in a productive tactical event; for example, a received pass should be immediately pushed into space for dribbling, a defense-penetration drill should finish with a shot on goal, a missed tackle should result in a recovery run by the tackler, and so on.

Tactics: Mastering cooperation with a partner, then a small group of supporting players, and finally with the entire team. Ideally, all tactical drills should be competitive and result in a win or loss.

Remember, there are specific tactical drills that can remedy any weakness in the play. A coach must isolate problems through careful match analysis, determine exactly which skills are involved, and build remedial practice sessions around them.

Drill Conditions

Most of the drills described in this chapter place conditions on the players. The conditions restrict space, time, or frequency of ball contact. The imposition of conditions allows the coach to modify basic drills to fit changing needs.

For example, the team's progress in ball-handling skills will demand increasingly tough drills. Drills can be toughened by using the same routines but confining them to smaller areas. This way, reaction time is reduced, demands on accuracy are increased, and repetition rate is stepped up.

It may be useful to increase the speed of a drill. This can be done by requiring more repetitions of an activity within a set time frame.

A common condition is a limit on the number of contacts with the ball in controlling it and completing a play. This is known as touch condition. For example, three-touch soccer requires a player to bring the ball under control with the first touch, position it for a pass or shot on goal with the second touch, and pass or shoot with the third touch.

It is not advisable to impose touch conditions on players who are still acquiring ball skills. They tend to lose confidence when required to give up the ball before completing the move they are trying to make. As they gain skill and confidence, touch conditions can be imposed; say, from four-touch to two-touch soccer.

Tactical Drills

At the entry and basic playing levels, tactical training is only moderately useful because players are still working on ball skills. To them, winning the ball and keeping possession take priority over what to do with it. Nevertheless, simple tactics can be taught to inexperienced youngsters through tactical drills that are extensions of skill-acquisition drills.

The tactical drills illustrated and described in this section are based on both individual and group tactics. Working with support players in the drills provides, in itself, a pressure situation. An error by one member of the group causes an interruption of the drill, so there is peer pressure to perform well.

PASSING AND MOBILITY DRILLS

These drills encourage players to run in support after they pass the ball. These fundamental drills do not include challenge pressure, but can include pressures from space, time, and touch conditions.

Two-player push. Two types of mobile push pass drills are shown in figure 33. In figure *a*, player A serves the ball to player B and runs ahead. Player B, who stays stationary, wall-passes the serve for A to collect. The drill reverses direction, with A taking as little time as possible to turn the ball around and serve it again to B. Players A and B exchange roles after several repetitions.

In figure *b*, player A serves the ball to player B and runs ahead. As A passes B, B turns the ball quickly and serves it ahead of A for him to run on and collect. The drill then reverses direction. Again, A's objective is to turn the ball around and serve it to B as quickly as possible while staying in motion.

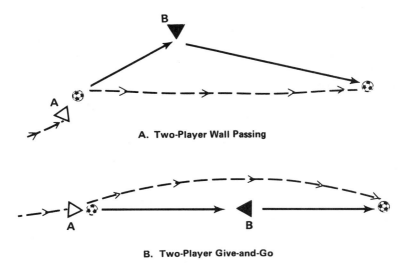

A. Two-Player Wall Passing

B. Two-Player Give-and-Go

Figure 33. Two-Player Push Passing Drill

Interchange weave. As shown in figure 34, two players dribble and serve through passes to each other while interchanging positions after each pass. The interchange is always made by the server behind the receiver.

Figure 34. Interchange Weave Passing Drill

Three-player layoff. This drill, as shown in figure 35, is performed with a group of three players. One player serves the ball while dribbling forwards. Two backward-running players take turns stopping the ball with one touch for the forward-running player to collect, and then they continue running backwards. The cycle is repeated several times, then the players change roles.

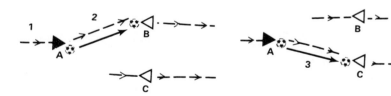

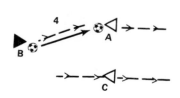

1. A dribbling, B and C running backward.
2. A serves to B on the run, B stops ball one-touch. B and C continue running backward.
3. A serves to C on run. C stops ball one-touch. C and B continue running backward.
4. B changes places with A or C and cycles continue until all three players have served several times.

Figure 35. Three Player Layoff Passing Drill

Short-short-long. Three players, arranged in line eight to twelve yards apart (fig. 36), exchange one-touch passes. An end player, on getting a short pass back from the middle player, sends a long pass to the other end, then switches positions with the middle player.

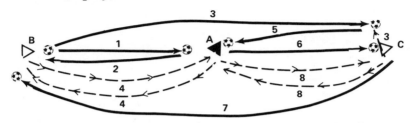

All One Touch:

1. B serves to A
2. A serves to B
3. B serves to C
4. A and B interchange
5. C serves to A
6. A serves to C
7. C serves to B
8. A and C interchange
9. Cycles repeat

Figure 36. Short-Short-Long Passing Drill

Four-queue give-and-go. This drill can be performed by the entire team. As shown in figure 37, the team forms into four queues. The lead player in a queue serves the lead player in any other queue, calling his name as he serves. The server then runs to the rear of the queue to which he just served. The receiving lead player serves under one-touch condition to any other lead player and runs to the rear of that queue. The sequence repeats through several cycles.

Hare and hounds. This dynamic, close-support tactical drill pits four attackers (hares) against two defenders (hounds) in a restricted area (grid). The drill develops a fine sense of triangular positioning in passing support for attackers, and in play anticipation for defenders (fig. 38).

The four hares are restricted to running between four markers (A to C, A to B, B to D, and C to D). The objective is for the hares to pass safely to each other while the hounds try to win the ball. A hound who wins the ball replaces the dispossessed hare between the markers. Since the hares may not leave the lines between the markers, the hare with the ball is forced to rely on exceptionally good receiving support.

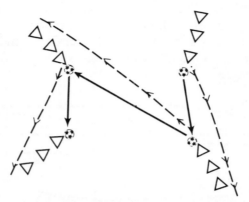

1. Lead player in queue serves to lead player in any other queue and runs to anchor position in that queue.
2. Receiver serves one-touch and repeats cycle.

Figure 37.   Four-Queue Give-and-Go Passing Drill

Hound 1 in figure 38a is in good position to challenge hare 1 for possession and to intercept a square pass to hare 2. Hound 2 has a good chance to intercept a through pass to hare 3. So, the best option is a square pass to hare 4, who is running toward marker C. In figure 38b, hound 2 has anticipated the square pass to hare 4, so the best pass option becomes a through pass to hare 3.

In hare and hounds, all hares should be aware of the best passing option. Only the hare in best support position should call for the ball. The hares should draw the challenger toward them before releasing the ball so that the challenger cannot easily challenge the receiver after the pass.

Three-on-one support. This drill forces close-support players to find open space quickly to receive square passes. One defender tries to win the ball from three attackers. The drill is best done in a grid; otherwise, the drill starts to spread out and lose its effectiveness. The players are free to move anywhere within the grid.

The drill must move fast, with the ball-winning defender quickly replacing the ball-losing attacker. To prevent the defender from intercepting a pass or being able to tackle:

1. The passer should always have two options for pass targets. For this to happen, the receivers should always be moving

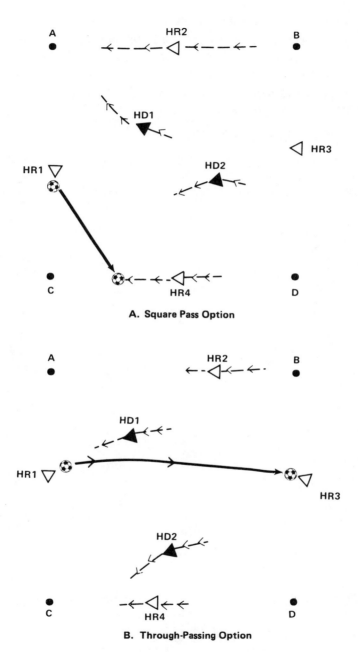

A. Square Pass Option

B. Through-Passing Option

Figure 38. Hare-and-Hounds Passing Drills

more or less square to the passer.

2. The fewer touches on the ball the better. If the drill is being done with more than two touches per play, the grid is too large or the players are loafing.

3. A potential receiver should never allow the defender to get between him and the ball.

PRACTICE GRID TRAINING

A typical practice grid is diagrammed in figure 39. It can be

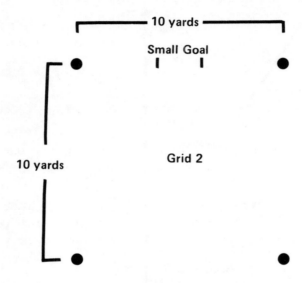

Figure 39. Practice Grid

used for a variety of effective tactical training drills. It can also be used as an arena for warmups and tactical drills that require boundaries.

One defensive tactical drill that uses the practice grid goes as follows:

1. Defender 1 controls grid 1 and defender 2 controls grid 2. Defender 2 never enters grid 1.

2. The dribbler enters grid 1. Defender 1 tries to contain the dribbler and tackle if necessary before the dribbler gets to grid 2.

3. If defender 1 is beaten, he must make a recovery run into grid 2, to get behind defender 2 as backup support. Defender 2 contains the dribbler until defender 1 is in backup support position, then tackles to win the ball. The dribbler attempts to score on the small goal at the end of the grid.

An offensive tactical drill using the practice grid goes as follows:

1. Two attackers enter grid 1 with the ball, against one defender. The two attackers are under two-touch restriction. Also, they must not shoot on goal.

2. The defender attempts to win the ball before the attackers penetrate grid 2. If the attackers do penetrate grid 2, they come under one-touch restriction and may now shoot on the small goal.

STRIKING SUPPORT

Pressure on the defense, pace acceleration, surprise, and determination are essential ingredients in putting the ball past the keeper. If the defense is poorly organized or the individual defensemen are weak, a determined and controlled run by a capable dribbler will usually produce a goal. However, if the defense is well organized and skilled, precise close-support passing will be needed to split the defense.

As the attack penetrates deeper into the striking zone, the pace must pick up and the passes must get shorter. Immediately before the strike, passing should be one-touch and rapid.

To develop the skills necessary to split the toughest defenses, forwards and halfbacks should be drilled under steadily in-

creasing speed demands. Two useful striking drills are illustrated in figures 40 and 41.

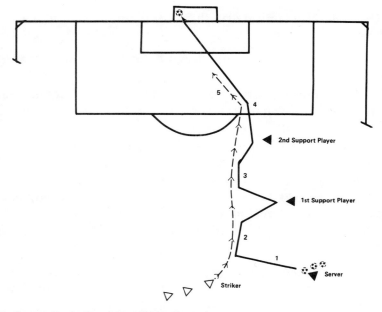

1. Server gives lead pass to striker at head of queue.
2. Striker collects ball, dribbles, and makes wall pass with first support player.
3. Striker collects ball, dribbles, and serves ball to second support player.
4. Second support player sends lead pass, weighted properly for striker to collect in
   penalty area and make first-time shot on goal no closer than penalty mark.
5. Striker follows up shot to collect fumble or rebound.

Figure 40. Central Striking Drill

Small-sided Games

Small-sided games can be very effective problem solvers. A
coach can design them with a particular tactical objective in
mind. Then, through continuous repetitions of the game with a
group of players, he can correct deficiencies as they occur.

There are so many variations of area size, team size, and conditions that only typical small-sided games can be described. It
is up to the coach to select the playing conditions that best fit
his players' needs. But two important principles of small-sided
games always apply:

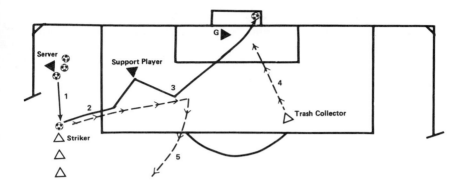

1. Server sends ball to striker at head of queue.
2. Striker dribbles and wall passes to support players.
3. Striker shoots on goal first-time with returned pass.
4. Trash collector puts pressure on keeper and finishes any bad shot or save.
5. Striker returns to end of queue and trash collector retreats and cycle repeats.

Figure 41. Cross-Goal Striking Drill

    1. The smaller the playing area, the greater the speed of the game and the need for precise ball control.

    2. If only one of the teams is being drilled to resolve a problem, always give the advantage to that team. For example, the defending team should be given the advantage of size or conditions when practicing defensive tactics. If the team being drilled is continuously frustrated by even combat, the objective of the drill will be lost.

    Small-sided games don't have to be played with a keeper. And, instead of a regulation goal, markers may be positioned about four feet apart and scores restricted to those shots that travel between the markers below marker height. In this way, scoring chances are cut down to about the odds of scoring against a keeper in a regulation goal. Alternatively, the goal could be widened to about six feet and the ball required to be dribbled through for a score.

One-on-one keepaway. This is an even contest, pitting one defender against one attacker. It drills individual defensive and striking tactics simultaneously. The defender wins by destroying a strike on goal. The striker wins by finishing with a shot on goal. The drill goes as follows:

1. Place a marker on the center spot of the field to serve as the goal.

2. Place the defender in the center circle and serve the ball to the striker outside the center circle.

3. The defender must quickly chase and contain the striker to keep him from penetrating the circle. The defender must not tackle and the striker must not shoot on goal until the striker penetrates the circle.

Two-on-one keepaway. This is an offensive drill, with two attackers teaming to keep the ball while one opponent tries to win the ball. It is a useful drill for teaching defense-splitting combinations. The drill goes as follows:

1. Construct a ten-yard square grid in which the contestants will play.

2. Serve the ball to one attacker. The attackers attempt to keep passing angles open, interchange passes, and keep possession of the ball. The opponent tries to cut off passes, tackle, and win the ball. On winning the ball from an attacker, the opponent switches roles with the attacker.

Three-on-three. A typical tactical small-sided game is three-on-three, pitting defense against offense on even terms. The drill goes as follows:

1. Set up a grid about forty yards long by twenty yards wide. Place a temporary regulation-width goal at one end. A soccer field penalty area is ideal, with the goal set up on one penalty area sideline as shown in figure 42. Mark off a defense area boundary about fifteen yards from the temporary goal.

2. Set up the following playing conditions: a time limit for the game, three-touch soccer outside the defense area, and no shooting on goal from outside the defense area.

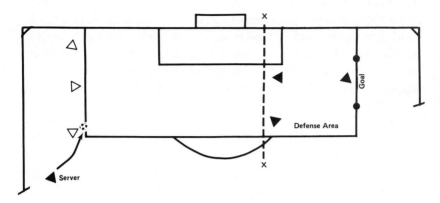

Figure 42. Small-Sided Game Using Penalty Area

3. Position the goalie and the two defenders in the defense area, and the three attackers at the opposite end of the grid.

4. Serve the ball to an attacking player. The defenders should immediately move out to cover the attackers running off the ball, contain the dribbler, and cut off passing angles. If the ball penetrates the defense area, one defender should be marking the most dangerous pass target (attacker nearest the goal), one defender must tackle the dribbler, and the keeper must provide backup support for the tackler.

5. The defense wins the game by winning the ball and moving it outside the defense area. (On winning the ball, the defenders should make use of the keeper by passing to him, moving out of the defense area, and letting him set up the counterattack.) The attackers win by scoring within the time limit.

Four-goal scrimmage. This game drills a team in space-making, close-support passing, and role changing (attack to defense and vice versa). The practice grid is diagrammed in figure 43. Team A defends the two yellow goals and attacks the two red goals, while team B defends the red goals and attacks the yellow goals. There are no goalies and no set player positions. Offensive tactical emphasis centers on switching attacks suddenly to the more weakly defended goal and decoying defenders out of position in order to score. Conversely, defensive tactics call for fast reaction to the offensive switch and denying passing space to the most dangerous pass targets.

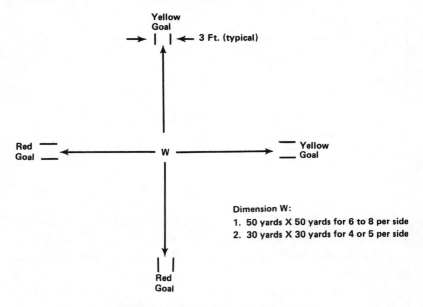

Figure 43.   Four-Goal Scrimmage Arena

Offensive three on two. This game is played on a quarter field. It drills defense-splitting tactics. It may be played into a regulation goal against a goalie, or into a four-foot goal without a goalie.

Three attackers start at midfield under three-touch condition against two defenders. The attackers win by scoring, with one bonus point awarded for each one-touch through pass. The defenders win by winning the ball, with five bonus points awarded for winning the ball outside the penalty area.

Offensive six on five. This game is played on a half field. One goalie and four field players defend a regulation goal. Six players defend a four-foot goal without a goalie. With condition variations, several offensive tactics can be drilled: (1) A dribbler must beat one challenger before passing the ball to improve improvisation ability. (2) A dribbler must sprint at least ten yards in support after passing off to improve support movement. (3) The six-player team must score with head shots only to improve air control and chipping.

Defensive three on two. This game is played on a quarter field. It drills quick repossession and counterattack.

Two attackers with a ball start at midfield, with no touch conditions, against three defenders in the penalty area. The attackers win by dribbling (not passing) into the penalty area. The defense wins by winning the ball and passing it back over the center line to a receiver in three touches or less.

Defensive six on five. This game is played on half a field. Six players (one goalie and five field players) defend a regulation goal. Five players defend a four-foot goal without a goalie. With condition variations, several defensive tactics can be drilled: (1) A challenger who is beaten must run to back up the next challenger. (2) A challenger who is beaten must chase and try to win the ball back before the dribbler plays it off.

Linkman desertion. This game is played on a quarter field with four-foot goals and no goalies. The drill is designed to increase the speed at which a team changes from defense to offense, and vice versa. The small-game sides are four-on-four, plus two free-agent linkmen. The game proceeds as follows:

1. The ball is served to team A. The two free-agent linkmen join team B to defend against team A.

2. When team A loses possession, either by scoring or losing the ball, the two linkmen join team A to defend against team B. If team B wins the ball in play, the game stops and the linkmen desert to team A before the game is restarted with a drop ball.

Scrimmages

The scrimmage is more involved than a small-sided game but still more manageable than a practice game. The team is evenly split and the halves play against each other. A regulation pitch should be used for more than seven to a side, half a pitch for smaller sides.

It will usually be advisable to impose touch conditions. For example, until the team is working comfortably together, it would be advisable to restrict practices to four-touch soccer. Or, if the team is concentrating on striking speed, two-touch condition in the attack zone is appropriate.

Other kinds of conditions can be imposed, depending on the skills and tactics to be drilled:

- Team may score only with head shots.
- Team may score only with volley shots.
- Players must sprint ten yards in support after they pass.
- Players must beat one opponent before they may pass.

Just as in small-sided games, the coach should stay close to the action and work on technical deficiencies as he spots them. When he sees weaknesses, he should "freeze" the players in position, reconstruct the moves, and have the players replay the moves properly. He must be sure to explain the disadvantages of the bad tactics (for example, lost opportunities for decoy runs, a communication breakdown in a restart, lack of depth or width in an offensive buildup, etc.) and the advantages of good tactics.

Practice Games

Practice games with other teams provide an advantage over those teams whose practices consist only of ball-skill drills, small-sided games, and scrimmages. Practice games allow a coach to see if his training program is paying off, to spot weaknesses in his players under pressure, and to experiment with lineup changes without worrying about losing a league match because of the changes.

Practice games should be scheduled with teams of similar capability. If the opposing team is too weak, it will not be able to apply meaningful pressure, and so weaknesses that need correcting will not show up. If the other team is too strong, the coach's team will be under too much pressure for him to have a chance to evaluate their potential.

Functional Training

The discussion of training so far has mainly covered the development of players as generalists and team members. But there are specialty skills that should be developed for specific playing positions. Most obvious are the specialty skills of the keeper, many of which are unique to that position. The art of developing specialty skills is called "functional training."

As a team progresses to successively higher levels of soccer, the need for functional training, except for the keeper, diminishes. This is because, in high-level soccer, all field players are expected to do everything well. Forwards should be just as skilled as fullbacks at tackling, fullbacks should be as capable at dribbling as forwards, and so on. However, no matter how fluid a team's system of play becomes, some players will be required to do particular things more often than other players.

GOALKEEPER

The four most important assets of a keeper are quickness, strength, agility, and determination. Determination must be continually encouraged by the coach. Strength can be built up during special fitness sessions and weight training. Leg strength is particularly important, as are arm and hand strength. Here are some examples of drills to sharpen a keeper's quickness and agility:

1. Goalie stands with his back to a server. The server rolls a ball by the goalie, who then pounces on the ball as fast as he can. A variation has the goalie facing the server and turning to pounce on the ball after it goes by.

2. The server bounces the ball behind the goalie, who must turn and catch the ball when he hears the bounce.

3. Goalie squats between two markers spaced six feet apart. A server throws a ball to the outside of the markers, which the goalie must leap and catch without touching the markers.

4. Goalie stands in the six-yard box facing a server behind the goal line. The server throws a ball to the goalie, who must turn, place the ball on the ground, and kick to a moving target man patrolling just outside the penalty area. A variation of this drill uses several pairs of players patrolling over that half of the

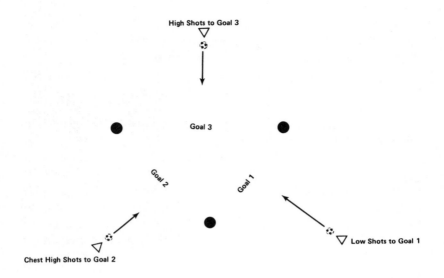

Figure 44. Goalkeeper Grid Drill

field with the target man among them; the goalie must get the ball to the target man either on an immediate short goal kick, a long goal kick, or a throw.

5. Goalie alternately covers each of three goals set up with three markers arranged in a triangle (see figure 44). One player sends him low shots, a second player sends him chest high shots, and a third player sends him high shots. The goalie must recover quickly from each shot and be ready in the next goal for the next shot without any pauses.

FULLBACKS

Most functional training for fullbacks is accomplished in defensive small-sided games, where fullbacks can drill on their clearing and overlapping functions. Sample drills include

1. A server chips balls from about twenty yards to the fullback, who heads the ball back past the server. In a variation, the fullback heads the ball to specified targets, calling the targets each time.

Pylons or extra balls can be used to mark off small goals for special drills.

2. In another variation of the above drill, the fullback clears the ball upfield or to specified targets with an instep volley kick.

3. Someone serves a ground pass toward a target beyond the fullback. The fullback slides to knock the ball away from the target.

4. A wing fullback serves a pass to his center half (see figure 45), who holds the ball while drawing a challenger towards it. Meanwhile, the wing fullback makes an overlapping run down the wing. The center half feeds a through pass for the wing fullback to run on and collect. (This drill ideally would start with the keeper throwing a serve to the wing fullback.)

MIDFIELDERS

Midfielders are expected to do everything the forwards and fullbacks do because they support the forwards on offense and the fullbacks on defense. They do have a specialty function called "linking," which means that the midfielders are responsible for making key ball distributions to the forwards in the attack zone once the ball has been received from the fullbacks. So two types of functional drills are required, one for speeding up switches from defense to attack and vice versa, and one for sharpening the decision-making process. Here are examples of two such drills:

1. The switching drill is similar to Four-Goal Scrimmage. Four markers form a ten-yard square, two adjacent markers of one color and the opposite markers of a different color. A ball is served to two pairs of midfielders in the grid. Each pair of midfielders defends one of the sets of markers. The midfielders score by winning the ball from their opponents and hitting either of the markers their opponents are defending.

2. In the linking drill, a midfielder faces a server about twenty yards away. Three receivers wait downfield behind the midfielder. The midfielder must bring down an air pass from the server with one touch, turn and maneuver the ball with the second touch, and serve the ball to a designated receiver with the third touch. The receiver should be designated while the ball is in the air from the server.

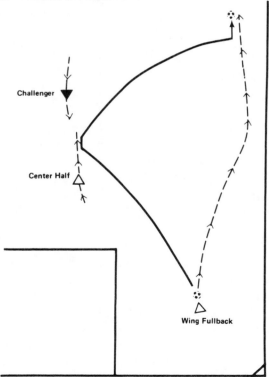

Figure 45. Fullback Overlapping Run Drill

FORWARDS

Functional training for forwards is covered by the striking drills described in "Tactical Drills." However, wingers frequently meet situations that need special training attention. Usually, the space in the corners of the field is not as well defended as the space in front of the goal under attack. So it is to the advantage of the wingers to use the space in the corners for carrying the ball while drawing the defenders away from the front of the goal. This way, they make space for the inside forwards or for themselves to cut into. Useful drills for achieving these objectives go as follows:

1. The winger dribbles the ball downfield, just inside the touchline, drawing a defender towards the ball. The winger feeds the ball back to a following support player, and they beat the defender with a give-and-go pass. The winger then dribbles toward the goal line and feeds the ball back and across to a central inside forward for him to strike.

2. In a variation of drill 1 above, the winger's support player cuts into the center following the give-and-go pass and receives the cross from the winger.

7

Frequently Asked Questions

The preceding chapters have outlined the common (and some uncommon) tactical maneuvers and problems step by step and drill by drill. This chapter will deal with the same tactics, but from a different perspective: the questions coaches most often ask at development clinics. This should prove helpful since in some cases the problem a coach wants to work on will involve several tactical factors, not to mention fitness and skills considerations as well. In other cases, the approach a coach should take will depend on age or experience levels. As discussed in chapter 5, Match Analysis, a coach has many variables to take into account when deciding how to improve his team's play. Perhaps by going over the most frequently cited problem areas, we will give the coach some practice in match analysis and a better idea of how to use the information in this book.

Some coaches feel that only game experience will solve these problems. This is not the case. Game experience reinforces game habits—good or bad. Sound training based on careful analysis of team abilities is the only way to suppress bad habits and develop good playing habits. With that in mind, here is commentary on the most commonly raised tactical questions.

"My players swarm around the ball."

This from a coach of eight- and nine-year-old boys. Some causes of this problem were described in chapter 3. The possible solution—scrimmages with touch conditions—may be

For young, inexperienced players, swarming around the ball is natural. Do not worry too much about a remedy. Players at this level should be having fun and concentrating on developing technique, not tactical skills.

too advanced for this coach's players. The first question should be: is the remedy worth the effort? If that team is relatively inexperienced, swarming is very natural. Exposing players that young and with that little experience to tactical training is putting the cart before the horse. They should be having fun, getting familiar with the game, and developing ball-handling skills.

A team with twelve months or more of playing experience per player should have the necessary level of ball skills to profit from rudimentary tactical training. In this case, scrimmages with the condition that all passes be longer than ten yards is about as rudimentary as you can get, but probably effective for this problem at that level. Players that age will not necessarily know how far ten yards is, so be sure to show them. If a pass is served less than ten yards, the ball turns over to the other team.

"Our opponents go through my defensive line like a knife through butter."

This from a coach of fourteen- and fifteen-year-old boys. The coach had four strong, fast backs with better-than-average ball skills. But there might as well have been only one player in the back because they literally were arrayed in a defensive line, with all the weaknesses inherent in a flat defense (refer to chapter 4 under Defensive Tactics).

Further questions put to this coach revealed that his back four did not press up behind the midfielders when their team was on the attack. So, when the ball turned over to the opposing team, there were no players to challenge the opponents' advance and slow them down, so the defense could build up.

Before any work is done on solving the group tactical deficiency problems, a hard look must be taken at the tackling capabilities of the back four. Tackling is really about two parts tactics and one part technique. The "when" and "where" of tackling are just as important as the "how" of tackling. The importance of backup support in the tackle is covered in chapter 3 under "Individual Tactics" and in chapter 4 under "Defensive Tactics." An effective tackling drill is described in chapter 6 under "Practice Grid." This type of individual training should be preliminary to larger-scale tactical remedies.

The "where" and "when" of tackling are as important as the "how" of tackling.

Any of several drills or small-sided games could be employed to solve the first part of the group-tactics problem (flat defense). The most direct approach is a defensive four-on-three small-sided game which recreates the defensive problem, then is conditioned to solve the problem.

Set up a grid in about a quarter of the field as shown in figure 46. Set up a zone across the width of the grid about five yards deep at the head of the defensive third of the grid. First, condition the game so that the four defenders must confine themselves in the five-yard zone at all times. Under these conditions, the attackers should have little difficulty setting up a through-pass attack.

Next, condition the game so that defenders D3 and D2 must

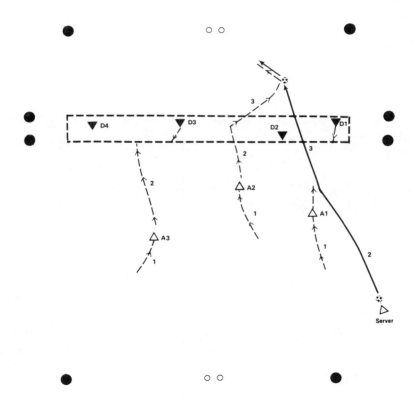

Figure 46. 4-on-3 Flat Defense Demonstration
Small-Sided Game

stay in back of the five-yard zone, and D4 and D1 must stay in front of the five-yard zone, until the ball is served (Fig. 47). Notice now the staggered defense, against which the three attackers struggle. Even though A1 is able to beat D1, he is under immediate pressure from D2. A cross pass to A3 could be easily intercepted by D3 (effectively, a sweeper).

The second part of the problem, failure of the backs to press forward on the attack, is better handled with a conditioned scrimmage. The only condition required is that for a team to score a goal, all players on the team must be in the offensive half of the field when the ball enters the goal; otherwise, no goal. This is a very strong incentive for defenders to press up behind the attack.

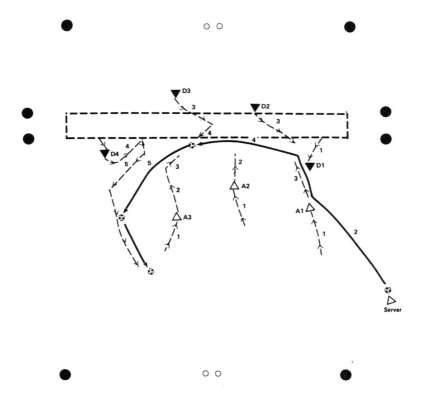

**Figure 47.   4-on-3 Staggered Defense Demonstration
Small-Sided Game**

"My forwards are afraid to shoot."

This from a coach of under-eighteen girls. Many chances for shots on goal were ignored during competition, with the ball in the center of the attack zone usually winding up on the wings instead of in the net.

The girls did not lack shooting skills under low-pressure conditions, but gave up the ball quickly when placed under pressure. The solution: the "turkey shoot."

The "turkey shoot" is a small-sided game that encourages first-time shooting on goal under pressure conditions. It can be played with regulation-width goals if they are tended by the regular goalkeepers on the team, or narrower goals if they are tended by stand-in field players. The goals are spaced about thirty yards apart for teenagers and about twenty yards apart for preteens. Each team has one goalkeeper and three or four field players. The idle players act as ball retrievers behind each goal.

Each game lasts for two to four minutes, and must be played at a fast pace. At the end of each game, the idle players replace the active players.

The games are played under one-touch conditions. A goalkeeper serves the ball to a teammate, who must shoot first time on the opposition's goal or pass one-touch to another teammate. Thereafter, any field player receiving a pass from another field player (even an opposing field player) must shoot first time on goal. The conditions of this game teach strikers to make quick decisions.

"My team always gives the ball to the other team."

This from a coach of eleven- and twelve-year-old boys. Although their passing was reasonably accurate, the number of turnovers to the opposing team was enough to cause losses of games that the team should have won.

The tactical problem here is not being able to judge when to release the ball. The ball is being released when the receiver is still closely marked by an opponent who should have been drawn away from the receiver before the pass was served.

A simple skill-development drill can be used to demonstrate to players the value of drawing an opponent before sending the

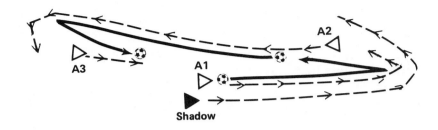

Figure 48. Overlap Decoy Passing Drill

pass. As shown in figure 48, dribbler A1 overlaps A2 with a defensive shadow player running closely in pursuit. A1, once the shadow moves out of range of A2, heel passes to A2. A2 dribbles toward A3 until the shadow catches up with him. A2 then overlaps A3 and, once the shadow player moves out of range of A3, heel passes to A3. The shadow player sprints to pursue A3, and so on for ten circuits. Then the shadow changes places with an A player.

The shadow must be required to follow the dribbler until the pass is served. If the dribbler does not overlap sufficiently, or he does not send the pass with enough weight, the shadow will be able to intercept the pass.

"My team has had only four shots on goal in the last two games."

This from a coach of thirteen- to fifteen-year-old girls. The ball had been in the attack zone many times more than the shots on goal frequency, but had been easily won by the defense.

The fact was that there had been little positive support from midfield because the halfbacks fed the ball to the forwards and stayed back to admire their distributions. The fullbacks also were guilty of low mobility on attack. A flat offense results because the ball tends to stay at one plane on the field for relatively long periods. There are three lines of bodies across the field: the fullbacks, the midfielders, and the forwards, who are struggling against the opposition to maintain possession of the ball. In between these lines of bodies is precious space in which to play productive attacking soccer.

Quite simply, these girls had no concept of playing the ball backwards to gain space, relieve pressure, and pull defenders out of position. An interesting and effective solution to this problem is a scrimmage with the single condition that each pass forward must be followed by a pass backward. A shot on goal would be made under the same condition as a pass; that is, it can be made only as a result of a pass back from a more forward position.

"My players will not pass."

This from a coach of twelve- and thirteen-year-old boys. The problem of not passing is common at that age because the players are just starting to feel very confident that they can dribble past any opponent on the field. At the same time, they have not yet fully developed group tactical awareness, such as the need for pass targets to be running off the ball. So the reluctance to pass on the part of the dribbler plus the unavailability of good passing opportunities result in continual loss of possession and a slow, monotonous style of play.

Properly conditioned scrimmages and mobile passing drills of the give-and-go variety will take care of this problem, but a word of caution. Too much remedial work in this area could have a counterproductive effect on the creative, improvising players on the team. There is a notorious lack of this kind of player, even at world-class levels, and care should be taken not to stifle a player's flair for taking one or two opponents on one-on-one if he is capable of doing it.

Several mobile passing drills are described in chapter 6 that are effective at the group tactical level, notably three-on-one support and hare-and-hounds. These should be used as warm-up preliminaries to a tightly conditioned scrimmage, where the conditions are that players are restricted to two touches on the ball and that some given number of consecutive passes (say four or five) between teammates constitutes a goal.

"My players are kick-ball artists."

This from a coach of under-sixteen girls. Kick-and-run soccer, whenever personal ball skills are lacking, is natural.

Creative, improvising players who can beat opponents consistently one-on-one under heavy pressure are hard to find, even at world-class levels. Be careful not to stifle this talent with rigid passing requirements.

Kick-and-run soccer is the natural consequence of underdeveloped ball skills. If players are not confident they can control the ball under pressure, their natural instinct is to kick it away as soon as possible.

Without the confidence of knowing they can control the ball, the natural instinct is to get rid of the ball as soon as possible under pressure.

This coach is observing a problem that plagues all coaches of youngsters who have not acquired the level of technique necessary to start concentrating on their tactical development. But there are drills that help develop ball skills while generating tactical awareness at the same time.

In this particular case, control-and-turn drills develop touch feeling with the ball while demonstrating to the players the value of immediately finding space with the ball. The lack of space in which to move the ball without challenge is the basic reason players become "kick-ball artists." A second reason for the panic clearance kick is purely tactical: the players have not been shown the value of placing the ball with one of their teammates rather than put it up for grabs with a high air-ball.

Figure 49 shows two control-and-turn drills that should precede functional training for distribution clearances. The pair of players shown in diagram A are under no pressure and are merely turning passes to their right or left with one touch, then sending a return pass with the next touch. Both the inside and outside surfaces of both feet should be used. At least half the drill time should be used in turning the ball with one foot across the body and using the other foot to send the return pass.

Diagram B extends the basic control-and-turn drill into a pressure drill. It involves more players, is more mobile, and includes challenge pressure. Player P1 sends a pass to P2 and sprints to challenge P2. Player P2 turns the ball one-touch into space, then sends a pass to P3. Player P2 sprints at P3 to challenge him, and P3 turns the ball into space. These sequences continue for many cycles. Drill pressures can be increased by shortening the distances between the players or by requiring the ball to be served in the air with a chip pass.

Figure 50 shows some basic set-pieces that can be used to develop a defender's distribution capabilities. In set-piece 1, a server sends a long through pass for the left winger. The right fullback has the job, under pressure from the left winger, of turning the ball back to the goalkeeper. (If the through pass were coming very fast, the right fullback could sell a dummy to the left winger and let the pass continue to the goalkeeper.)

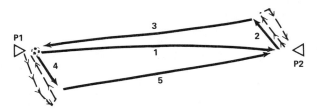

A. Pairs Drill for Developing Control-and-Turn Touch

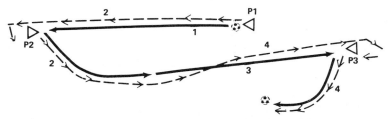

**B. Small-Group Drill for Opening Up Passing or Dribbling Space
Under Challenge**

Figure 49. Control-and-Turn Drills

In set-pieces 2 and 3, a center fullback and then a left fullback are added to provide close lateral passing support and crossfield lateral passing support. Note that the crossfield passing support is very valuable because the attack has developed up the left side of the field, and that side is loaded with opposing players. Consequently, the opposite side of the field is underloaded with opposing players and ripe for exploitation (refer to chapter 4 under "Pressure in Team Tactics").

In set-piece 4, a center forward and a supporting center forward have been added to the picture. The center forward's task is to shut down the center fullback as a pass target for the right fullback and to make a long pass to the left fullback difficult. The supporting center forward's task is to attract a long clearance for counterattack possibilities.

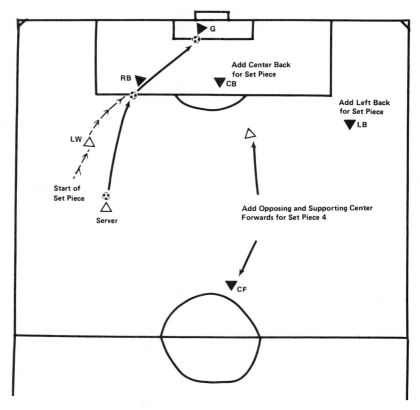

Figure 50. Set-Pieces in Functional Training of a Defender

System Mobility

On paper, systems of play look neat and practical. However, in match situations their starting pattern lasts for only a few seconds following the kickoff. Experienced teams will maintain the very general pattern of their system during play (even though players may interchange positions). Less experienced teams will quickly lose the starting pattern of the system through lack of mobility or, conversely, through excessive mobility. The importance of system mobility is covered in greater detail in chapter 3.

Glossary

Attack area - The third of the soccer field in front of the goal being attacked. Sometimes called the "attack zone."

Ball carrier - The player dribbling the ball.

Ball skills - The techniques used by individual players to control the ball.

Blind side - An area on the field of play that cannot be seen by a given player or official.

Built offense - A systematically developed attack, as opposed to a counterattack.

Center forward - Central player of the forward players.

Center fullback - Central player of the defenders.

Center half - Central player of the midfielders.

Challenger - The player who confronts the ball carrier for the purpose of tackling him or containing him.

Challenge support - The defending player immediately behind the challenger for the ball.

Chase-and-delay - The defensive tactic of sprinting towards a ball carrier and slowing him down by applying containment pressure.

Clearance - The defense's act of sending the ball away from their goal area.

Close support - Moving near a dribbling teammate to give him a passing option on attack or providing challenge support on defense.

Close-support passes - Serves to nearby pass targets.

Collect - To receive and control a pass.

Compactness - The tendency of a team to move with the movements of the ball so that total team offensive and defensive pressure is distributed around the ball.

Condition - Any tactical restriction placed on players during practice (such as the number of touches on the ball, size of the play area, or time limit).

Contain - A defensive tactic in which a challenger confronts a ball carrier without tackling him in order to slow him down or confine him in the same general area.

Counterattack - A fast attack on the opponent's goal immediately following repossession of the ball, without benefit of an offensive buildup.

Cover - To keep watch on an opponent with the objective of challenging him if he receives a pass.

Deadball - (1) A ball that is not officially in play. (2) A ball that is officially in play but not moving.

Decoy run - Movement off the ball by a player to lure an opponent away from the ball carrier or a pass target.

Defender - Usually a fullback, but can be any player who is engaging in defensive tactics.

Defense area - The third of the soccer field in front of the goal being defended. Sometimes called the "defense zone."

Defensive buildup - Sequences of play during which the defending team prepares to win the ball back. Generally consists of containing the ball carrier while other defenders move to cover or mark the ball carrier's pass targets.

Depth - The length (upfield and downfield) of a defending or attacking player formation as compared to its width (crossfield). For example, a deep defense (sometimes called a "staggered" defense) is usually longer than it is wide.

Double pass - (1) A give-and-go pass where the return pass is delayed until the receiver is clear of a defending player. (2) A pass in which the server touches the ball in one direction to throw a challenger off balance in that direction, then passes the ball to a receiver in the other direction.

Double teaming - A tactic consisting of two defenders working side-by-side to challenge the ball carrier (as distinct from challenge support, where two defenders challenge in series).

Dribble - To keep possession of the ball and propel it along the ground with the feet.

Drop kick - A kick executed by dropping the ball from the hands onto the kicking foot.

Economical training - Combining ball-skill, tactical, and physical-fitness training to achieve match fitness.

Far-post cross - A pass from the wings that is aimed at an attacker located near the goalpost on the opposite side from the passer.

First-time shot - A shot made on goal from a pass without a first touch to control the pass.

Finish - To shoot on goal.

Fullback - Defensive player protecting the defense area.

Functional training - Drills designed for training specialty functions; for example, goalkeeping, wing play, linking, etc.

Funneling back - A tactic used by a team to organize a defense between their goal and the advancing opponents.

Give-and-go - (1) Give-and-go soccer is a style that features continuous passing and running off the ball in support of the receiver. (2) A give-and-go is a short pass to a receiver followed by a sprint into nearby space to collect a return pass.

Grid - A marked area of a selected size and shape in which drills are held.

Halfback - (See **midfielder**.)

Half volley kick - A kick executed by contacting the ball with the foot just as the ball contacts the ground.

High-pressure defense - Defensive tactics characterized by man-to-man coverage and challenge pressure mounted as soon as the opponents win the ball.

High-pressure offense - Offensive tactics characterized by fast counterattacks as soon as the ball is won with little or no offensive buildup.

Improvisation - A delaying tactic by the ball carrier to allow his teammates to build up an offense. Usually consists of running with the ball into space across field or opposite to the direction of attack, or interpassing with a teammate at midfield.

Inside forward - A forward player who plays on either side of the center forward, if a center forward is used in the system, or any central forward player.

Inswinger - Corner kick or cross-goal pass that swerves towards the goal.

Integrated passing - The tactics employed by a passer and receiver working together as a unit.

Interchange run - (1) Lateral (crossfield) movement of a player past the ball carrier with the objective of collecting (or faking to collect) a pass from the ball carrier. (2) Crossfield exchange of positions between players (for example, a position exchange between an inside right and his right winger).

Interval training - A physical conditioning program using action that simulates match pace; that is, short bursts of intense activitiy interspersed into longer periods of medium-paced activity.

Killer pass - A through pass (usually long) that leaves the defense no chance of catching the striker who collects it.

Layoff pass - (1) The ball carrier leaves the ball in place and continues, while the receiver runs and collects the stationary ball. (2) Any short pass used to relieve defensive pressure on the ball carrier.

Lead - The distance advantage one player has over his opponent in the direction of play.

Lead pass - A pass served into the space ahead of a running player so that the running player can collect the ball without breaking his stride or changing speed.

Linkman - (See **midfielder**.)

Low-pressure defense - Defensive tactics characterized by zone defense and organized defensive buildup.

Low-pressure offense - Offensive tactics characterized by organized offensive buildup prior to attempt at defense penetration.

Man-to-man defense - Defensive control of an assigned opponent, rather than defensive control of an assigned area on the field of play. As opposed to "zone defense."

Mark - To stay close to an opponent with the objective of intercepting a pass to that opponent.

Match - A competitive soccer game.

Match analysis - Systematic isolation of strengths and weaknesses in a team by watching and analyzing its performance in competition.

Match fitness - Condition of a player when his physical condition, ball skills, and tactical skills are at their peak and he is effective at his team's competitive level.

Match pace - The rhythm and speed of a soccer match.

Match pressure - The pressures on players during a soccer match, such as challenge, space limitation, audience attitude, fatigue, match pace, teammate attitude, etc.

Match-related pressure - Pressure imposed on players in practices that simulate match pressure.

Midfield - Generally, the middle third of the soccer field (see **preparation area**).

Midfielder - Player who is responsible for control in the central part of the soccer field, between the forwards and the fullbacks. Sometimes called halfback (because of his field position) or linkman (because of his primary function of distributing passes from his fullbacks to his forwards).

Mode - The state of the game; either defensive, offensive, or ball out of play.

Movement off the ball - (See **running off the ball**).

Near-post cross - A pass from the wings that is aimed at an attacker located close to the goalpost on the same side of the field as the passer.

Offensive buildup - Sequences of play during which the attacking team prepares to score a goal. Generally consists of delaying forward progress of the ball at midfield while the off-the-ball forwards move to the attack zone and find or create weaknesses in the defense.

Offside - An infraction of Law XI whereby an attacker does not have two or more opponents between him and the goal he is attacking when the ball is played towards him by a teammate.

Offside position - The field position of an attacking player, whereby he is in the opposition's half of the field and he has less than two opponents between himself and the goal being attacked. (Note: being in offside position is not an infraction in itself until in the referee's opinion the player takes advantage of that position.)

Offside trap - A tactic performed by defenders who place an attacking player in offside position just before a teammate advances the ball.

Outswinger - Corner kick or cross-goal pass that swerves away from the goal.

Overlapping run - Movement of a player downfield past the ball carrier with the objective of collecting (or faking to collect) a pass from the ball carrier.

Own-goal - A ball accidentally sent into his own goal by a defender to score for the opposing team.

Pass target - A player who is a potential pass receiver.

Patrol - Slow-paced movement of a player as he maneuvers for effective field position.

Patterned run - Any purposeful offensive movement, either on or off the ball, with the purpose of opening up dribbling or passing space.

Penetration - The act of beating the defense preparatory to a strike.

Pitch - The field of play.

Playmaker - A player who creates playing opportunities for his teammates.

Porous defense - A defense which is easy to beat because it is poorly organized.

Practice grid - Any confined area constructed especially for drills, such as two adjacent squares for penetration drills.

Preparation area - The middle third of the field, in which offensive or defensive buildup usually occurs. Sometimes called the "staging" area or "preparation zone."

Pressuring - Keeping pressure on an opponent.

Progressive training - A training program that increases in skill and fitness requirements only after players can handle current requirements.

Push pass - A short serve made with the inside of the foot.

Recovery run - (1) Chase made by a dribbler after an opponent who has just won the ball from him. (2) Chase made by a challenger after a dribbler who has just beaten him. (3) Chase made by a player to his regular field position after a play has taken him away.

Remedial training - Training that is specially designed to eliminate a skill or fitness deficiency and bring a player up to par with his teammates.

Restart - Putting the ball back into play after it has gone out of play (such as a free kick, throw-in, etc.).

Restriction - (See **condition**.)

Running off (without) the ball - Running an an active supporting role while not in possession of the ball, such as being a pass target or decoy.

Running off (without) the ball - Running in an active supporting

Scrimmage - Informal practice game, usually played between two halves of the same team.

Selling the dummy - Faking to intercept a pass, then letting the ball continue to a nearby teammate with the objective of drawing a challenger to the site of the fake and away from the nearby teammate.

Service pass - Any type of pass sent to a player who has worked off the ball to achieve a particular objective (for example, made an overlapping run into good scoring position).

Serving - Passing.

Set-piece play - A tactic involving particular rehearsed moves by specific players, usually for restarts.

Short corner-kick - A pass by the corner kicker, usually on the ground, to a nearby teammate for him to shoot on goal.

Short goal-kick - A goal kick restart served to a teammate just outside the penalty area, who returns the ball to the goalie for him to drop kick clear.

Small-sided game - A practice game between two teams of up to six players each for the purpose of drilling one particular tactic.

Split the defense - To create an opening in a defense for penetration purposes.

Square pass - A pass that travels fairly laterally (across field) to the passer.

Staging zone - (See **preparation area.**)

Striker - The player who scores or attempts to score (usually applies to an inside forward, but not exclusively).

Striking - The act of scoring or attempting to score a goal. Sometimes called "finishing."

Sweeper - A free defender whose job is to support his teammates by denying running space to attackers behind his teammates. Sometimes called "libero."

System - Field formation of a team or functional unit of players.

System mobility - The way in which a team, or functional unit of players, tends to move on the field of play in relation to the movement of the ball.

Tactics - Short term plans by individual players, groups of players, or a team to execute a soccer play.

Technique - (See **ball skills.**)

Through pass - A pass that travels downfield past the defense for a teammate to run on and collect.

Timed run - A run started by a player at the last possible moment, to avoid detection by opponents.

Total soccer - A form of soccer requiring every player on a team to perform any tasks expertly under match pressures.

Touch - A player's sensitivity in making contact with the ball with the objective of controlling or sending it.

Touches - The number of contacts a player makes with the ball in receiving it and controlling it.

Touch condition - The number of contacts a player is restricted to in practices.

Trap - To stop the flight of the ball and bring it under control.

Trash goal - A goal scored through the mistake of the defense (such as a fumble by the goalie or a clearance rebounding off a player).

Two-touch soccer - A game in which players may contact the ball only twice before passing or shooting (that is, receive the ball with one contact and pass with the next contact).

Volley kick - A kick executed by contacting the ball with the foot while the ball is in flight.

Wall - A closely knit line of defenders set up to block a free kick on goal.

Wall pass - A type of give-and-go pass where the receiver rebounds the ball back to the passer behind the passer's challenger.

Weak side - The side of the field that has the least defensive coverage.

Weight - Speed at which a passed ball travels. (A properly weighted pass is one that is slow enough for the receiver to collect without losing control but fast enough not to be intercepted.)

Width - The width (crossfield) of a defending or attacking player system compared with its depth (upfield or downfield). For example, a wide (or flat) defense is wider than it is deep.

Winger - A forward who plays primarily at the outside edges of the playing field.

Wings - The outside edges of the playing field.

Work rate - The amount of work a player puts into his game.

Zone defense - Defensive control of an assigned area on the field of play, rather than defensive control of a particular opponent as in man-to-man defense.

Recommended Reading from

World Publications

Manual for Youth Soccer by Alan Maher
All the information you need to produce a successful youth soccer team is here, including planning practice sessions, sample drills, and systems of play. It covers items other books on soccer fail to mention, like team-reference communications, questions to ask the referee, how to scout your opponent, and now to operate a soccer tournament. Paperback, $1.95.

Soccer Basics by Eric Sellin
Outlined are fundamental principles of the game which the newcomer to soccer can use as a foundation for coaching youth soccer. Topics like how to fill a roster, player positioning, how to best utilize a player's ability, basic offensive and defensive formations, strategies and tactics are all discussed in simple nontechnical language. Paperback, $1.95.

The Basic Soccer Guide by Bobby Moffat
Included are all the necessary skills, strategies, practice drills, and style pointers from a former professional soccer player. The 33 exercises in **The Basic Soccer Guide** explain the basic skills of kicking, heading, dribbling, controlling, tackling, goalkeeping, shooting, and throw-ins. An appendix includes the complete rules of the game. Paperback, $3.50.

The Inner Game of Soccer by Eric Sellin
This is the ideal referee's handbook. **The Inner Game of Soccer** describes the actual game situations. There is a thorough analysis of the laws, practical tips on referee's signals, suggestions on pregame formalities, summary of high school and college rule variations, techniques, complete FIFA laws. A must handbook. Hardback, $7.95.

Soccer World Magazine
Soccer World is the magazine designed for soccer players, coaches, and enthusiasts. There are articles covering all aspects of the sport including major matches, playing strategies, and equipment evaluation, plus interviews with players and coaches and tips on conditioning and instruction. For beginners to professional competitors there's much. One year (6 issues) $7.50.

Available in fine bookstores and sport shops, or from:

World Publications, Inc.

Box 366, Mountain View, CA 94042.

Include $.45 shipping and handling for each title (maximum $2.25)